ceramic creations

By
ROBERT FOURNIER

ceramic creations

Photographs by J. M. Anderson

Contents

Introduction

Clay is an abundant material found the world over, so it is not surprising that its history as a creative medium is as long and as varied as the history of art itself. The fascination of forming objects from clay has persisted for over 6,000 years and continues to fascinate artist craftsmen today. While the techniques of the potter have remained much the same, the role and aim of the creative potter have changed.

It is no longer necessary in this technological age for the craftsman potter using hand methods to form the common everyday utensils used in every home. Modern production methods are now used to make dishes, bowls, mugs, pitchers. Today, the creative potter is closer to the painter and sculptor. He has at his disposal the best examples of ceramic creativity down through the ages, plus the greater technological knowledge of our time and the freedom to combine techniques and to find new forms and excellence within the medium. He can turn his attention to the creation of ceramic sculpture, to architectural pottery, to wall decoration, and, if he chooses, to the production of beautiful and utilitarian ware.

Anyone who has held clay in his hands and felt its responsiveness to his slightest touch has known the urge to explore the possibilities of this creative medium, to give form to the clay, to create new and fascinating shapes, textures, designs. To utilize all existing knowledge of clay, fire, color, and glazes, and to push our knowledge beyond these bounds—that is the goal of the ceramist.

This book is for the potter who already has a working knowledge of clay and glazes and who wishes to expand upon and utilize his knowledge in new and creative ways. It is also for the trained beginner, who recently embarked on the adventurous discovery and pleasure of pottery making and ceramic creation.

The book is a re-examination of pottery techniques—pinch pots, slab building, coil building, pottery dishes without molds, modeling, pulling handles, raku, and glazing—for those who want to perfect their workmanship and progress to new levels of self-expression.

Illustration 1

How to narrow the neck on a large bottle. With your left hand inside and right hand outside, use the knuckle of your forefinger. Always throw and narrow with a minimum of flesh in contact with the clay.

I. The Techniques of Throwing

There is an ancient Egyptian symbol showing the God Khnum forming man on the potter's wheel. This is a vivid illustration of both the antiquity of throwing clay at the potter's wheel and of the apparent life and growth of clay as it spins between the fingers of a skillful potter.

For many centuries after its invention, the wheel held sway over all other ceramic techniques. With the rise of industrialization that took place during the 18th century in the Western world, the wheel was demoted to a mere turntable for making pots for the biscuit or plaster mold. In many country places, however, the humbler type of pot—flowerpot, casserole, bread bin or cider jar—continued to be thrown on the wheel, but today these country potteries and potters are all but gone.

In their place has arisen a more self-centering

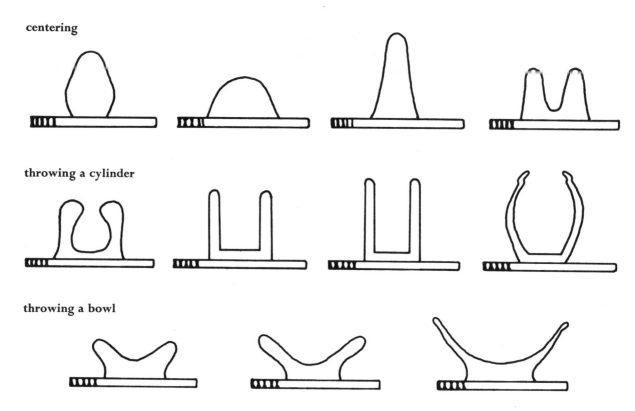

throwing a cylinder

throwing a bowl

Illustration 2
These are the main outlines that a clay ball takes under the hands of a skillful potter at the wheel—centering, raising a cylinder, and throwing a bowl.

Illustration 3. How to trim the foot of a bowl in leather-hard condition. Clean-cut shavings show the clay is neither too hard nor too wet.

conscious and aware potter, experimenting with form, using the thrown shape sculpturally, or producing everyday crockery imbued with personality and humanity.

THROWING

The effortless simplicity of throwing at the wheel comes only with practice and the development of sensitivity of touch and sympathy with the clay. It is a difficult craft to master, but the pleasure that comes from perfect control of the clay on the wheel is well worth the time and application.

The best way to learn to throw is through direct instruction from a capable and experienced potter. Studying at a ceramic school or with a competent potter is highly recommended. But, in addition, there are certain guides and standards which can help you check your work and judge your progress.

There are many types of potter's wheel. Some, called "kick wheels," are turned by the potter's foot, kicking a large horizontal flywheel attached to the base of a vertical shaft. At the top of the shaft is a wheel head. This is the surface upon which the clay is formed. Other types of wheels are operated by a treadle.

Most potters' wheels in use today are either kick wheels or motor-driven wheels. Electric wheels are less tiring, can be operated more quickly, and are favored by many potters, but the beginner should start on a kick wheel if possible.

Shaping the clay on the potter's wheel is what is called throwing. It is essential for throwing that the clay be of the right type. It must be highly plastic, yielding, and responsive, with enough body to retain a shape, such as a tall cylinder with thin walls, without collapsing.

Clay to be used at the wheel—or in any other manner—must always be properly wedged. The kneading of clay into a mass of uniform consistency is called "wedging." You must cut and wedge the clay at least 20 times until there are no air bubbles showing on the cut surface, before shaping the clay into balls. To start with, make a dozen balls of baseball size and keep them wrapped in plastic or a damp cloth until they are ready to be used.

Illustration 4
A sculptural construction made of thrown pots cut into rings and sections and assembled on a slab base. Chris Wilson, Maidstone College of Art.

In addition to the clay and wheel, all you require for throwing are a few tools: a bowl for water, a sponge, potter's knife, pricker, and a supply of bats.

CENTERING

Do not begrudge the time spent in centering. The clay is centered when it has been pushed into a perfectly symmetrical disc right over the center of the wheel so that it runs true. Until centering is mastered no progress can be made. Apply a firm and steady pressure in one direction only. Do not press on both sides of the clay at once.

Centering is almost instantaneous once the knack has been learned. In centering—as in all

9

steps of the throwing process—it is of prime importance to grip and release the clay steadily and progressively. Any sudden movement is fatal to the pot being formed.

OPENING AND PULLING

Once the clay has been centered properly, it is "opened" to form the bottom of the pot. Push your right thumb downward into the center of the ball of clay.

Illustration 5
Simple, well proportioned lidded jar. Stoneware, 6 inches high. Elsie Murray, Chaucer Institute.

The bottom is shaped by pulling from the center outward. Use a pricker to determine the thickness of the bottom. The walls of the pot can then be drawn up and shaped to form the desired pot.

In these operations, throw with a minimum of flesh in contact with the clay. Two fingers will give as much control as ten, are less likely to tear and twist the wall, and produce less slip. Those potters who are frequently pictured covered to the elbows in wet clay may be photogenic, but they are poor examples of good throwing techniques and should not be followed.

Rims should not be sharp or mean. On a bowl, pot, or casserole the rim can be a major feature of good design. A good rim will minimize warping and will help the glaze adhere properly to the pot.

TURNING

Turning or trimming is required to pare excess clay from the pot when it is leather hard. It is usual on bowls where a footrim is required, but trimming is not always necessary in the case of jugs, beakers, etc. These are best cut tidily from the wheel, with the base left flat or slightly tapped inward with a tap of the fingers.

FORM

Finally, let your pot forms be well defined. A cylinder of good proportions is preferable to a squat barrel. You will soon discover that a beaker or a bowl which is both good to look at and efficient to use presents as great a challenge as an abstract or decorative pot. A typical design problem is the balance of handle, lid, and spout of a teapot. Each potter must solve a given design problem in his own terms.

A pot is essentially a container. Esthetically it is a container of space. Let this space be generous.

2. Pinch Pots

Illustration 6

Various forms and decorations of pinch pots. Left to right: bowl from single ball of clay, decorated with paper stencil and slip; double pot with added neck and foot; small pebble form decorated with sand and iron dust beaten into surface; larger form sponged with slip and glaze.

Making pinch or "thumb pots" is almost instinctive whenever anyone picks up a piece of clay. Pinch pots can be made without the use of any pottery equipment.

The only requirement is a fairly moist, plastic clay—either earthenware or stoneware, buff or red. Grog may be added, but, if used in excess, some plasticity will be lost. If cracks appear on the clay's surface while you are working, smooth over immediately.

MAKING A SINGLE POT

To make a single pinch pot, roll the clay into a ball, the rounder the better for a symmetrical shape. Hold the ball in one palm and start to press the thumb of your other hand centrally into the lump, turning it with short, steady movements as the thumb penetrates. When within $\frac{1}{4}$ inch of the base, grip the pot between your thumb (inside) and fingers (outside) and begin to squeeze the walls to an even thickness, revolving the pot about $\frac{1}{2}$ inch between each "pinch."

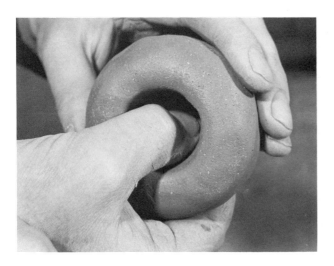

Illustration 7

To begin the pinch pot, press your thumb into the center of a ball of clay.

Illustration 8
The nearly completed pinch pot with smooth and even walls.

Do not try to thin the wall haphazardly. Keep up a steady, rhythmic and even series of movements. This will result in a craftsmanlike finish and save much time and effort in the long run. Work round and round in a spiral towards the neck of the pot. If a shoulder is required on the finished pot, keep the mouth as small as possible. In most cases a generous lip will be required either for joining or to give firmness to the structure.

Do not stand the pot on its base while the clay is still soft. Rest the pot on its side or rim,

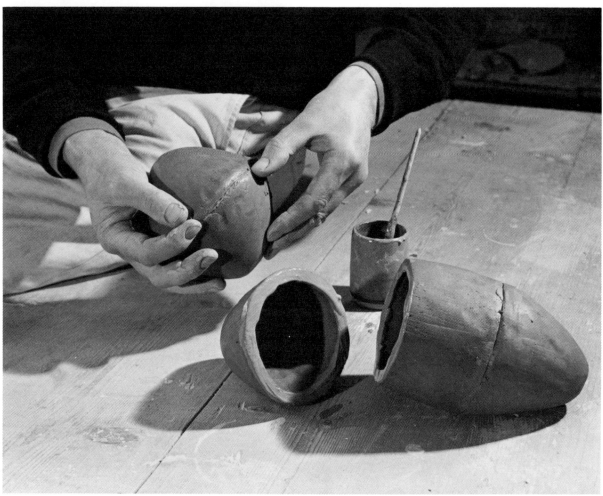

Illustration 9
To join two small pots, as at the left, score, lute with slip, and then smooth over the seam. At the right, a "collar," which was made by punching a thumb right through a ball of clay before smoothing the walls, has been joined to a bowl.

Illustration 10
Roll a double or joined pot to smooth and perfect
form. The damp ring on the worktable shows tracks
of the pot.

or place it in a "mold" such as a biscuit bowl. To control the height/width relationship, sit the pot in the palm of your hand (as in Illustration 8) and squeeze slightly around the circumference after each turn.

COMPOSITE POTS

With practice, single pots and bowls up to 6 inches can be achieved. By joining two or more pinch pots of this size, quite large and impressive pieces can be built. The final form of the composite pot may be the traditional circular plan or it may be asymmetrical through any section, but thought must be given to the final design *before* any of the individual parts are made.

Obviously, two pots with inturned rims are unsuitable for joining, and component pots are usually in the form of deep or shallow bowls which must have rims of the same diameter. A hollow "collar," made by pushing the thumb right through a ball of clay before thinning the walls, can be inserted between two bowls to

provide greater height (Illustration 9). Flatten the rims by gently beating or inverting onto a wooden surface. If the pots are soft and liable to be easily distorted, leave them to harden before joining.

To join, score the rims and smear liberally with slip (liquid clay made from the same clay as the pots). Press the surfaces together, wipe off surplus slip, and then work the clay up and down across the join to smooth.

The form can now be rolled, worked, patted, or beaten to the desired shape. The contained air will maintain a more or less constant volume and any considerable alteration in total size, such as softening or flattening a curve, must be preceded by making a small needle prick in the wall with a needle or tool to permit some air to escape. If the pot is to remain a closed form, a small prick must be made to prevent the pot from exploding in the firing.

Illustration 11
A composite made from three pinched forms is gently beaten into shape. Always beat to shape on the profile of the pot, constantly turning to show a new profile.

13

Illustration 12. Several types of necks complete pinch pots. Left, neck opening with inward sloping cut; center, long neck formed around a brush being luted with slip onto the pot; right, a pinched out neck or "frill."

Illustration 13. How to make a foot on a pinch pot by (left) indenting base with thumb and (right) by adding a coil to the base.

14

Illustration 14. Pinch pots lend themselves to irregular forms. Start with an egg-shaped ball of clay to form these asymmetrical pinched shapes.

FINISHING—NECKS AND FEET

To form the neck, a simple opening can be cut in the top of a nearly closed pinch pot, but there are many other possibilities. The rim can be pinched up like the top of a seed pod. A short neck can be made from a ring or coil, or a longer neck can be formed around a pencil or brush, shaped and luted on with slip.

A foot in the form of a coil or ring can add lightness and elegance, or a stem can be left when pinching the lower section. In cases where a foot will not be added, make a dent under the base so that the pot will stand firmly.

DECORATING

Any ceramic technique may be used in the surface decoration. Beating in red grog or iron dust will give attractive results on pebble-like shapes. Brushing with any metallic oxides will create interesting effects, or slip decoration may be used on green or biscuit ware. In any case, the approach to surface decoration should be simple and direct. The subtleties and slight irregularities of shape inherent in the technique are often sufficient in themselves, and, of course, the biscuited ware may appropriately be glazed or left partially unglazed.

OTHER APPROACHES

Although the pinch pot is often thought of as a simple form, it can be used with great sophistication to form a wide variety of ceramic ware and sculpture. Figures, animal forms, and piggy banks are often made from pinch pots (Illustration 14), and many potters have brought the pinch pot to great heights. Well grogged pinch pots also are suitable for sawdust flowerpot firings or for raku. (See Chapter 10.)

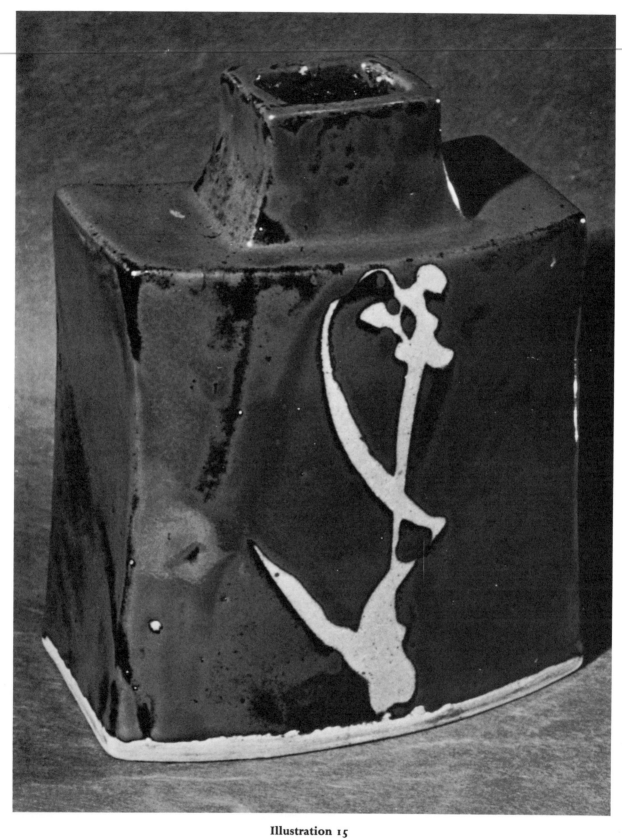

Illustration 15
A curved slab pot by the Japanese potter Shoji Hamada. A fine example of strong, sophisticated slabwork appropriately glazed.

16

3. Slab Pots

Building pots from sheets of rolled-out clay contrasts strongly with the technique of making pinch pots. But like pinch pots, slab work can be done with little equipment. All that is required are: a rolling pin, a rolling cloth, potter's knife, ruler and a good firm surface, such as a table top or artist's board. Circular cutters, T squares, and a plane are optional extras.

There are three main types of slab pot: pots with all flat surfaces, pots with curved walls, and cylindrical pots.

SLAB POTS WITH FLAT SURFACES

First make some sketches of your slab pot and decide on its size and proportions. Make a note of the precise measurements or cut "patterns" for the individual parts. For slab pots, the clay to be used should be grogged to prevent warping and undue shrinkage.

Start by rolling out the clay on the table with the rolling pin, using guide sticks to mark the thickness of the clay. For a medium pot 9 inches high, use $\frac{3}{8}$-inch sticks for the main faces and $\frac{1}{2}$-inch sticks for the narrower walls. Base and top should be $\frac{3}{8}$ inch in thickness. Prepare extra slabs for experimenting with feet, necks, etc. Lightly indicate the shapes of pieces on the rolled-out clay and cut larger than finally required, allowing for both the later trimming and for the shrinkage in drying and firing.

At this stage any impressed decoration can be marked on the clay surface. On a scrap slab, try any tool, odd piece of wood, or other handy implement for interesting impressed marks, or

Illustration 16. Design impressed on plastic clay with bamboo tool.

17

Illustration 17. How to cut the sides out of stiffened clay, keeping all angles right angles.

Illustration 18. Lute the sides of the slab pot to the face, smoothing a coil into the angles.

18

use a ball of string or a cotton reel to press into the clay or to roll across it.

Once impressed, incised or otherwise decorated, put the slabs aside to stiffen. If the pot cannot be finished immediately, cover the slabs with plastic until your next work session. If not too wet, the pieces can be laid one on another.

When the clay has stiffened enough to be handled without flopping, cut the slabs to precise measurements with a square. Be careful to cut with the knife held upright. Angled cuts will lead to poor joins, cracking, and warping.

Now assemble the walls, laying a $\frac{3}{8}$-inch piece face down and, using plenty of slip made from the same clay, join the $\frac{1}{2}$-inch side slabs to it. A narrow coil laid into the angle and smoothed over will help to ensure a strong join.

The base can be inset when three walls have

been joined, or the completed pot may be luted down onto the base slab. Luting down is the process of adhering the pot to a completed base using slip as an adhesive. An open pot will be stronger if a top slab is used and the opening is cut through it. This is especially true of flowerpots or plant containers where the long side is liable to warp inwards.

Necks and shoulders can be thrown, luted onto the pot when stiff, and cut to shape. A shoulder also can be built up from triangular sections. For a lamp base a short neck on the top slab is useful to hold the fitting. It can be cut from a $\frac{1}{2}$-inch or thicker piece of clay, or a coil can be used.

Oval or oblong-cut slabs or strips slightly inset under the base of a slab pot will greatly improve the appearance and finish.

A knife or plane can be used to obliterate

Illustration 19
Two ways of joining a base. On the left, the base is inset between the sides after being accurately cut to size. At the right, the completed walls are joined to a flat base.

Illustration 20. Suggested tops for slab pots. Left, an inset slab cut with an oval opening. Right, a cut coil.

signs of joining and to level the surface. Slightly beveled or rounded corners are best.

All-over decoration on the sides of a pot is likely to be damaged in the forming process, and it is more practical to be satisfied with plain or simply textured sides or with a strip of decoration down the center.

Impressed decoration can be inlaid with pigment, slip or glaze, or conversely, rapid strokes of pigment with the side of a wide brush will color the face and leave the impressions relatively clear. This can be done at any stage, on the dry clay, biscuit or unfired glaze.

Illustration 21. Inverted slab pots showing oval and rectangular foot-rims.

Illustration 22
Rolling up a cylinder slab prior to joining. Note the oblique cuts for the join.

SLAB POTS WITH CURVED WALLS

Fundamentally, the same principles of forming and decorating hold for pots in which two or more surfaces are curved. Obviously, the clay rolled out to make the curve must be plastic enough and the pot generally must be assembled upright.

SLAB POTS FORMED AS CYLINDERS

To make a cylindrical slab pot use a core. This can be in the form of a rolling pin or a cardboard cylinder such as paper toweling is wrapped on or is used to send calendars or other papers through the mail.

Wrap a sheet of fairly stiff paper around the core and fasten it with an inch of tape. Roll out the clay and cut to the height of the pot. Make an oblique cut along one edge and, using the rolling cloth, wind the sheet of plastic clay around the core. Mark where the cut edge touches the face at the completion of the revolution. Unwind an inch or two, and make another oblique cut along this line so that the two edges will overlap. This technique is shown in Illustration 22.

Score, slip and join, and roll the two edges firmly together. Stand on end and remove the core, leaving the paper in the clay cylinder. The paper will help the cylinder stand up, but will not split the pot as the clay shrinks. It can be removed as soon as the pot is able to stand on its own. Ideally, the cylinder should now be left to stiffen, along with enough sheet clay to make the base and top.

The base, top, neck and foot of the cylinder slab pot can be treated the same way as slab pots with straight walls.

Illustration 23
A stoneware slab cylinder pot by Sheila Fournier,
appropriately decorated and glazed.

GENERAL ADVICE

During firing, slab pots have a habit of curving toward the elements of an electric kiln due to the greater shrinkage of the hot surface near the elements. Slab pots can be fired on their backs or sides in biscuit or glaze firings. In firing a slab pot that has glaze on its face, you cannot, of course, glaze the surface on which the pot rests on the kiln shelf.

Proportions of height, width, and depth are all-important and, in general, an oblong shape is more interesting than a square one.

The slab pot is highly suitable for a lamp base. On slab pots built for this purpose, cut a hole in the leather-hard clay near the base for the wiring.

While beginners should start with slab pots approximately 9 inches high, very large pots can be built up by the slab method, or several pots can be joined to form tall and exciting composite pots. When making large, composite pots, do not attempt to hide the joins, but instead make them a feature of the design.

The more or less neutral surfaces of a slab pot invite decoration of many types: applied, impressed, scored, resist, painted, etc. In the field of form and design a little imagination and invention will suggest many variations on the more straightforward slab pots described here.

4. Modeling

Ceramic modeling is modeling which can be fired without the previous use of molds or casts to form hollow pieces. It implies the use of those ceramic techniques which produce a comparatively thin, even wall of clay free of air pockets.

Modeling can also be done by making a solid form and hollowing it out or by modeling over a paper core, but there are hazards in both these methods. The solid piece, subsequently hollowed, must be fired very slowly to avoid breakage and hollowing is a tedious process, while modeling over a paper core often leads to excessively thick walls. Sophisticated and involved forms can be achieved by pottery techniques alone, but it is best to start modeling with simple forms and exercises.

There are four principal methods of making a hollow form through modeling: slabwork, thumbing or pinching, coiling, throwing. All four methods may be used alone or in combination, but each technique imposes its own character. Indiscriminate mixing of methods may lead to a lack of unity in the finished piece.

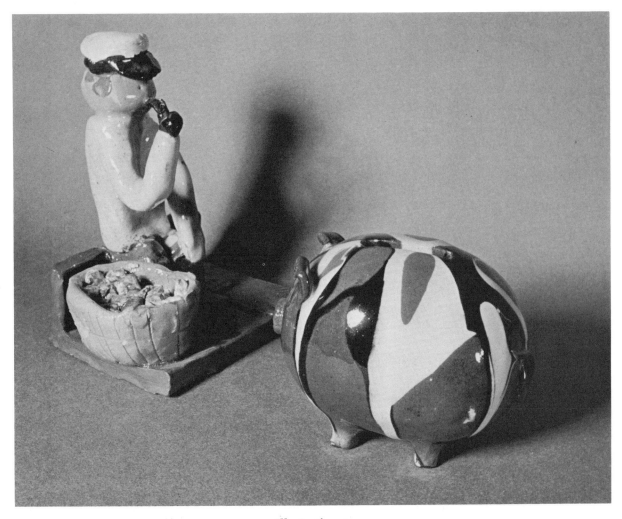

Illustration 24

Simple, hollow modeled forms—a small figurine and a traditional piggy bank, and glazed earthenware fired.

23

THE RULES

An understanding of the properties of clay will help you to form suitable and durable modeled pieces.

• All clays shrink in drying and again during firing. If soft wet clay is, therefore, applied to dry clay, tensions and cracks will result.

• Unless the clay is wet and soft, one piece will not adhere permanently to another simply by pressing them together. Use a dab of slip or water at every join. The exception is the technique of coiling, and even here a slight moistening between the coils of an asymmetric or involved form will ensure stability.

• Air and water expand with heat. Bubbles or pockets in the clay will explode during firing, and this includes the almost imperceptible layer of air which may be trapped if one flat area of clay is laid over another. The core of moisture liable to remain in a thick piece of clay, even when it appears dry, will form steam of great volume resulting in an explosion similar to the effect of a miniature bomb. Three-quarters of an inch is the recommended maximum wall thickness.

• The clay body has a direct bearing on drying. A close, dense, plastic clay or a fine-grain red clay will dry only slowly and, therefore, the maximum wall thickness of pottery made from such clays should be $\frac{1}{2}$ inch. All pieces made from such clays should also be given at least one week's drying time before firing. Some fireclays and other coarser-grain bodies will allow the escape of moisture more readily, but any clay can be "opened" by the addition of grog, i.e., ground pottery biscuit. Grog comes in various grain sizes, its use determined by the potter's requirements. But any grog which will pass through a 30-mesh sieve will give life and "bite" to the clay. Up to 30% grog by weight can be damped and wedged into a clay body.

• The limitations of modeling are inherent in the strength of the clay and its behavior in the kiln. These must be considered in any model calling for areas of support. For example, an extreme attempt at the impossible would be a dancer modeled unsupported "sur les points." Even realistic modeling of the four legs of a horse would be precarious, whereas the judicious thickening of an animal's legs or the choice of a recumbent or other more suitable poses are less artificial solutions to the problem of support. Even better is the stylizing of your subject into a more or less compact or self-supporting form. This will lead to more individual and creative work.

Another approach, and one naturally favored by potters is to start from a pot shape, such as a pinch pot, a tall thrown shape, a slab, cone or cylinder, or from several pots which can be cut and joined together. A great deal of recent work from American and European potters starts from the general concept of a "pot," but only as a means to invented form. The result can be interesting, but sometimes is an uncomfortable hybrid.

According to Bernard Leach, dean of British potters, there is a fine distinction between pots and sculpture. In a talk on contemporary American pottery, he said that if careful examination revealed even a small hole on top, then the work could be a pot, if not then it was "something else."

Illustration 25
Two pinch pots being smoothed over at the join.

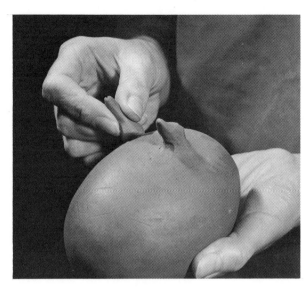

Illustration 26
Small pellets of clay are applied with dabs of slip to a pig model and then are fashioned into legs.

PINCHED FORMS

For practical considerations start with the simplest technique—that of joined pinched pots. By careful beating and modeling of the basic shape, together with suitable additions, various somewhat chubby creatures can be fashioned. The traditional piggy bank is the most obvious and often the most successful. The fact is, of course, that pigs are not round and fat, but that is how most people think of them. The egg shape or oval can be adapted to making fish, owls, and gourd or stonelike shapes.

PIGGY BANKS

To make a piggy bank, start by preparing two well-wedged balls of clay. The clay should be fairly plastic and soft. Half a pound is a good weight to start with, but with practice larger pieces can be handled.

Make two pinch pots from the balls, with even, not too thin walls, with openings of a similar size, and with flattened rims about $\frac{1}{2}$ inch wide. The curve should not exceed a half sphere or a difficult "waisted" form will result. Actually, it would be more accurate to describe these as two pinched bowls.

Next moisten the rims with slip, bring them together, and work over the join until it is smoothed out. It is also wise to score the rims before applying the slip.

Then apply ears, snout, legs, and tail. Add eyes and other details. Once the legs have been added, it will be necessary to support the piggy bank under the belly with a wedge of clay while the piece is drying. This will equalize the weight and prevent too much strain on the legs. In fact, the piece can be biscuit fired on the support.

Decoration of the finished piece can vary. The traditional "Sussex pig" had its back dipped in marbled slip (see Illustrations 28 and 29). A majolica treatment of a tin glaze painted with oxides also is popular. The flowers that are so often painted on piggy banks, it is interesting to note, can be traced back some 4,000 years to Egyptian hippo models which were decorated with stylized water plants.

If the piggy bank has been fashioned out of a stoneware body, a textured or carved surface

Illustration 27
Ears being applied to the pig model. Note the slab of clay supporting the body.

25

can be sponged over with a dark glaze. If the surplus is then cleaned away from the surface, the glaze left in the crevices will enhance the effect of the pattern.

Other glaze effects are possible. Only a section of the animal shape or an abstract shape may be dipped in glaze to give contrast and interest, or glaze can be poured over the form, perhaps giving the pot a sharp twist to give life to the dribbles. All glazing techniques need to be carried out cleanly and directly.

MODELING WITH SLABS

One of the simplest and most suggestive shapes to work with in modeling is the cone. It lends itself easily to forming a great variety of figures from bishops to angels.

Start by rolling out a sheet of clay. The thickness of the clay slab will depend on the size of the piece and the rigidity of construction required. The average thickness is between $\frac{1}{4}$ and $\frac{1}{2}$ inch.

Use a template of cardboard or paper to mark the dimensions of the cone. Cut with a knife or any implement that is handy. Then score, lute with slip, join the edges, and apply any other additions needed to create the model you have in mind.

The cone can be made from a slab without support, or it can be wrapped around a stiff paper core. As with all shapes made over a mold of any sort, the core must either be soft enough to crinkle up as the clay dries or it must be removed before the clay begins to shrink.

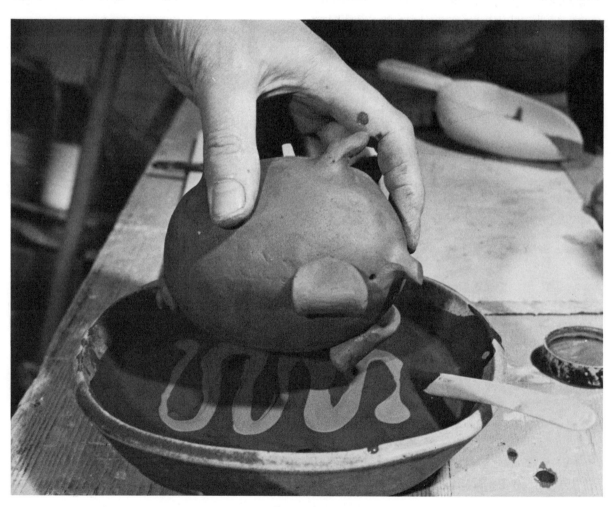

Illustration 28
Leather-hard, the figure is dipped into a small bowl half-filled with slip into which a contrasting slip has been dribbled in a wavy motion. Slip can also be applied to biscuited pot.

26

Illustration 29
The dipped pig with a pattern on its back. Stripes can also be applied to biscuit with glaze and wax resist.

Illustration 30. Partially glazed and fired piggy bank.

27

Illustration 31. A double pinched form is gently beaten into a flattened oval to form a fish.

Illustration 32. The flattened shape getting its "scales" with impressions formed by a wooden modeling tool.

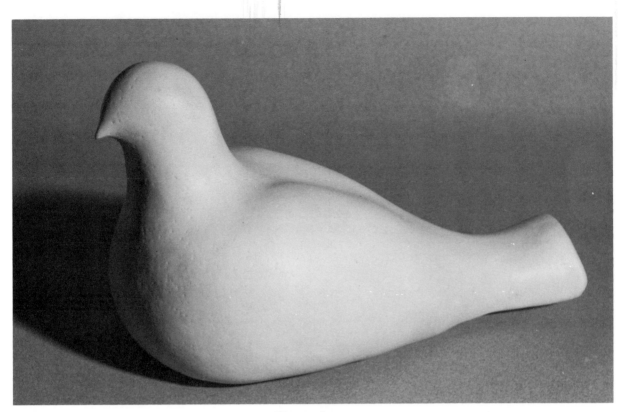

Illustration 33
A dove, 9 inches long, formed from joined pinch pots and modeled. By Frank Brown.

Illustration 34
Two pigeons modeled by Rosemary Wren in unglazed stoneware with fired pigment and small areas of brushed glaze, 7 inches long.

29

Illustration 35
An elegant group of figures based on the simple cone. Variations come from placement of detail, position of heads and arms.

Two layers of paper can be used to form the core: the inner one of thin cardboard or heavy paper, the outer of newspaper or bond paper. Remove the inner core as soon as the shape has been formed. The outer core will provide support while the clay stiffens. The thinner paper will give as the clay shrinks and may be left for a time or even fired in the biscuit.

But for immediate and lively shaping of the figure, let the cone stiffen to the point where it will stand but is still bent easily. A slab laid between two boards or on a plaster bat will achieve this state quickly. Slower and more natural drying on a wooden surface is the more desirable method, provided you have the time to wait.

Almost any clay body can be used for slab modeling, from a smooth earthenware body to

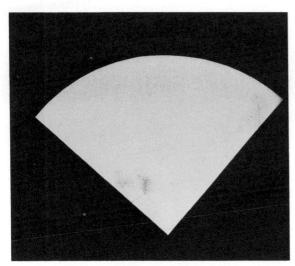

Illustration 36
Use a cardboard template to mark the dimensions of a cone on a clay sheet.

some red or other clay. A good red clay has high plasticity and is suitable for earthenware firing; however, earthenware clay can sometimes also be improved with the addition of 10% fine sand or grog.

The cone shape is a comparatively rigid and versatile foundation for direct pottery modeling. It can be adapted to many uses and can assume many variations of proportion and character. Each of the elegant figures in Illustration 35 utilizes the cone in a simple way. The proportions of the basic cones are tall and slender and immediately suggest the general character of the figure before a single detail is added.

As you work with slabs, other arrangements of simple, basic hollow shapes will occur to you. Make several versions of each shape, leave them to stiffen a little, and then begin to experiment. Cut, deform, build, join. Try numerous variations.

a highly grogged stoneware clay. For stoneware firing, it is advisable to add some sand or grog to the clay body. Avoid the white, so-called modeling clays, which feel like soap, have no grip or character, and are readily available at most pottery supply houses. If you are unlucky enough to "inherit" some of this type of clay body, wedge in some sand or grog and perhaps

Illustration 37
How to cut the cone slab with a knife, piece of nylon thread, or any suitable implement.

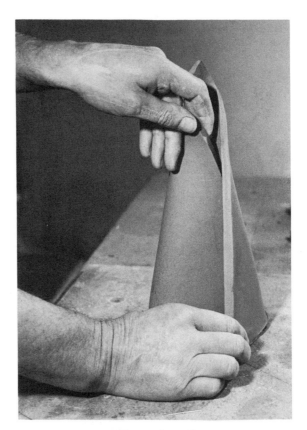

Illustration 38
The cone in the first stage of modeling.

31

MODELING A LION FROM SLABS

The accompanying illustrations (39 through 46) show the principal stages in the modeling of a lion with rolled-out sheets of clay.

The first step is to make a small mock-up to determine the general character and stance of the creature. This is important to make before a large-scale project is attempted. Although the final form may depart from the original in the details, the mock-up is invaluable in clarifying the idea for the project. As the final photograph

Illustration 40. A template is designed from the mock-up.

Illustration 41. A sheet of clay is rolled out and the template design cut.

shows (Illustration 46), the style of the mane was altered. The rather lumpy coils of the mock-up were replaced by more sprightly forms cut from slabs. This had the unifying virtue of continuing the technique used in the main body.

From the mock-up a "template" is worked out, leaving some leeway for later cutting, if necessary. The principal "lion characteristics" emphasized are: the strength of the shoulder as opposed to the more slender haunches, and the lion's loping gait, suggesting both speed and caution. The front legs consequently were thickened to almost triangular shapes. Note the simple, clear curves which are varied in length and quality.

The template was next laid on a sheet of grogged clay rolled to a thickness just under $\frac{1}{2}$ inch. The shape was cut with a needle awl. The sheet of clay, originally rolled out on hessian, was transferred to a board and allowed to stiffen a little. To transfer a large sheet of clay, slide the hessian onto a board, lay another on top and turn the whole "sandwich" over, gripping the two boards firmly together. The hessian, now on top, can be peeled off.

Next, mount a cardboard cylinder on two coiled supports. These are preferable to solid clay supports as they can be compressed under pressure and yet are strong. Then gently lift the cut-out clay sheet, draping it over the cylinder. Press the cylinder down until the "feet" just touch the board. The model is now left to dry until it will just stand on its own.

When the slab is dry enough to take its own weight, the cylinder and supports are removed. The rear end is now carefully squeezed into a narrower form and the whole body is given a slight curve. The dangers of collapse or splitting at this stage are obvious, but the additional liveliness which this twist imparts to the whole figure makes the risk worthwhile. It would have been possible to support the front half of the lion at this stage as in Illustration 45.

One of the coiled supports was lengthened to take the weight of the shoulders while working on them. Next, the mane was added, using cut-out shapes rather than rolled ones as originally conceived, with due regard to the growth-directions of the hair. The face also was reconsidered and re-worked, again using the slab technique and with a suggestion of heraldry about the interpretation which seems to fit well with the stylized mane.

Illustration 46 reveals the completed figure. Note that the tail was laid across the body. A free-standing tail has little chance of survival. It could equally firmly have been laid down the back of one of the legs, but this would have

33

interrupted the line. The model—17 inches long and weighing 10 pounds—was successfully stoneware fired 2282° F. (1250° C.) without support, the only precaution being a liberal sprinkling of alumina under the feet so that the creature could shrink without dragging or gripping the kiln shelf. The edges of the mane were brushed with manganese oxide, and the whole figure covered with a thin application of a buff glaze.

Illustration 43. The lion is allowed to dry slowly.

34

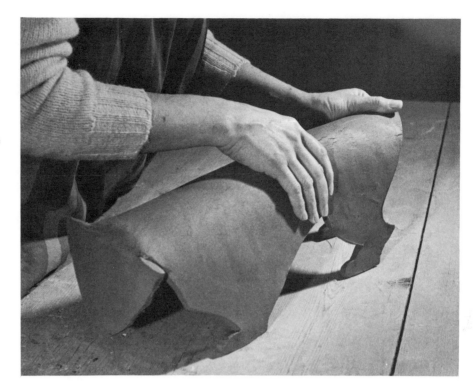

Illustration 44. When the slab is dry enough to take its own weight, the cylinder and supports are removed.

Illustration 45. The mane is formed through the addition of thin slab cut-outs. Coil supports should be replaced when adding mane so that pressure in this process will not cause body to collapse.

Illustration 46
The final modeled lion decorated with a manganese oxide wash under a buff glaze, and fired to stoneware temperature—2282° F. (1250° C.).

MODELING WITH COILS AND THROWN FORMS

The building of hollow figures also can be achieved by means of coils of clay. Coil building lends itself to the forming of both symmetrical and asymmetrical shapes which adapt well to modeling.

If you have a wheel, experiment with thrown forms. Quite a variety of thrown shapes can be utilized for models, either substantially as thrown or cut, joined, and pressed.

In addition, you can combine the four modeling methods to achieve your design.

TOOLS

A wooden spatula tool is perhaps the most useful modeling tool. It will cut, smooth, model, and impress. Wire loop tools are more limited in scope but often valuable. A kidney-shaped metal scraper, a strong needle awl and a small penknife are all useful, as are emery paper, combs, brushes (including cheap, stiff paste brushes) and sponges for smoothing and decorating.

FINISHES

The model can be left as plain biscuit, especially if made in red clay (terra cotta), but at earthenware temperatures 2012–2102° F. (1100–1150° C.) it will tend to get grubby in time. Throughout the ages, figures in pottery, stone, and metal, have been colored with un-fired pigments and this is still done by some modern sculptors.

Unglazed stoneware 2152–2372° F. (1200–1300° C.) is resistant to dirt, and before firing can be brushed or dabbed with a wide variety of slips and pigments—or even metals, such as copper and iron filings. A scored or textured surface can be "inlaid" with glaze by first sponging it in and then wiping the surface clean. It is, in fact, a good idea generally to wipe over the whole surface with a watery glaze and then to sponge it clean again. The glaze will fill holes and crevices and prevent the rather dead and dusty look that biscuit sometimes assumes.

In modeling, where there is no need for watertightness, glaze can be used in a freer and purely decorative fashion, applied with a brush or by dipping and pouring.

For the glazing of earthenware, a honey-colored glaze is recommended to intensify and unify slip decoration. Oxides to which water has been added to form a wash may be applied either on the raw, nearly-dry clay so that they are fixed by the biscuit firing, or else brushed on top of a white (tin) glaze as soon as the applied glaze is dry. A clear glaze can be used over pigments, but the results often lack sparkle and contrast.

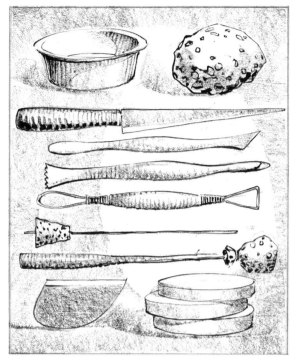

Drawing by Louis Di Valentin, from "Practical Encyclopedia of Crafts."

Useful equipment for ceramic modeling.

5. Coiled Table Lamps

Illustration 47

Lamp fashioned with earthenware coils, finished with white tin glaze over which color has been spun.

The coil method can be used successfully to make many varied shapes. One of these is the cylindrical coiled table lamp.

A cylinder is a straightforward shape and a good one on which to learn to coil. It has several advantages: The form is not as likely to sag out of shape as a full-bellied pot; it takes a shade well; and it is particularly suitable for carved decoration.

Care should be taken when designing the lamp base to consider the proportion of height to width. Generally speaking, a tall and fairly slender shape is advisable, although for a bedside or small table lamp, a squat form, wider than it is high, can be attractive. The height and type of neck also will radically affect the character and proportion of the finished lamp.

The clay used will depend on the way the lamp base is to be fired and glazed. The lamp in Illustration 47, for example, was made of an earthenware clay body and glazed with a white tin glaze over which color was spun.

THE BASE

Work out the relative height-to-width proportion and then decide on the actual size of the base. Cut a circle of stiff paper to the size of your base. Make a small ball of clay and beat it out with the palm of your hand onto the paper until it is about ⅜-inch thick and covers the circle. Reverse and cut the clay to the size of the paper, as in Illustration 48, then turn it back again so that the paper is underneath and you are ready to begin building the wall of the pot. The object of the paper circle is twofold: it will help to prevent the base from spreading unduly while the pot is being built, and it will stop the clay from sticking to the bench or to the turntable.

Illustration 48. Starting
the lamp with flattened
circular base.

ROLLING THE COIL

This is an apparently simple action which, nevertheless, often gives trouble to beginners. Round coils of an even thickness will not only improve the appearance of your work, but will also make the actual building and control of form much easier. The following hints may prove helpful.

1. Have your clay fairly soft but not sticky.

2. Give yourself plenty of room in which to roll the coil.

3. Cut your clay from a block with a wire and shape it roughly with your hands as in Illustration 49.

4. Roll with a long even movement from the

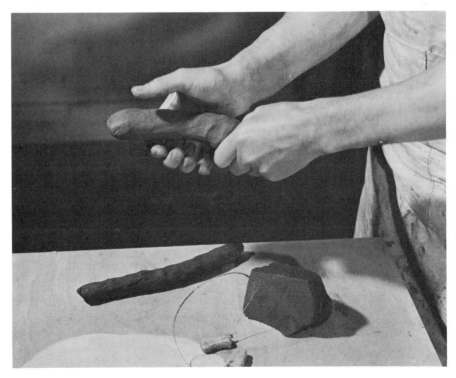

Illustration 49. Cutting
and roughly forming the
coil.

39

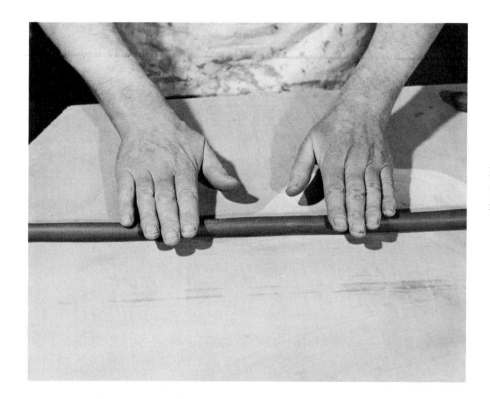

Illustration 50. Roll coil, with long, even movements.

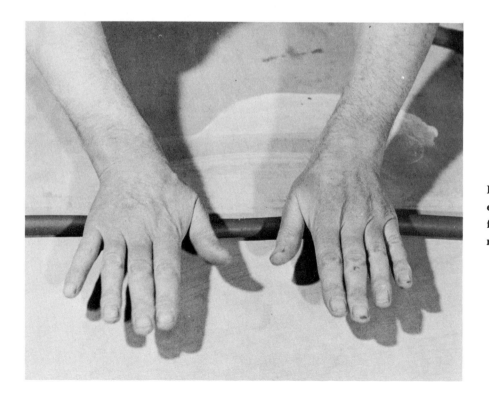

Illustration 51. Use your entire hand—palm and fingers—to form rounded solid coils.

Illustration 52
Fastening the first coil on the base. Use your thumb to smooth the clay vertically inside and out.

shoulders, your hands held flat and fingers together.

5. Use *all* of your hand—palm and fingers, as in Illustrations 50 and 51.

6. Start to roll with your hands side by side and move them apart as the coil lengthens. Inspect the ends of the coil occasionally to see that it is not developing a hole down the center.

At the start you will probably find that the coil insists on being oval. As soon as this happens, stop rolling and tap the coil back nearer to a circular shape and then continue. The flattening is due either to uneven or flabby pressure or to a short and jerky movement. An hour or so of practice should result in adequate coils.

COILING

The first few coils should be made carefully as they must bear the weight of the pot.

Roll them to a thickness of $\frac{1}{2}$ inch and as evenly as possible. Make a ring or coil to the size of the base, pinching off or cutting the ends at an angle so that they can be lapped at the join. Do not use a sponge at any stage: Coiling

is the one exception to the rule that clay must be slipped before joining.

With your thumb or finger pull a little of the surface clay downward or at a slight angle across the join between coil and base, inside and outside, as in Illustration 52. When all signs of the junction have been covered, the clay can be smoothed over with a horizontal stroke, but it must be stressed that all the effective work is done with the vertical pull. Continue to build up the cylinder by adding more coils, keeping the rings of equal size so that a cylindrical form is maintained.

Often it is helpful to make each ring a trifle smaller than the one below since the action of joining tends to squeeze the coil and so lengthen it.

There are two common methods of applying the coil. One is to make a coil of the required size, joined and complete, which is then laid on the pot and worked in. The second variation is to "feed" the coil on as the thumbing down progresses, nipping it off when the circuit is completed. There is a third system whereby the whole coil is used up each time, forming a spiral where it overlaps. This method is not recommended, for it creates an uneven wall thickness, and the shape is difficult to control.

Illustration 53
The partially formed, smoothed coiled lamp base. By placing the cylinder on a banding wheel, left hand can remain in a fixed position. Constant contact thus helps maintain even thickness.

Illustration 54
Two possible necks for the base—one hand-built, the other thrown on the wheel.

MAKING THE NECK

The neck of the lamp base may take many forms, from a simple $\frac{1}{2}$-inch hole in a flat top to a graceful thrown neck. If you do not wish to resort to the wheel, rings can be coiled onto a flat top, cut with pastry cutters, made freehand and luted on with slip, or squared.

In any case, it is advisable to buy the fittings to be used before finishing the lamp base so that you can be sure that the hole is suitable. Both a cut top and a thrown top can be seen in Illustration 54. The thrown top is shown on a completed lamp in the carving picture (Illustration 57). It is thrown like a squat bottle with the base removed. It is possible to go right down to the wheelhead when throwing, but the top is easier to remove and handle if a floor is left in. This is cut away later. To make a cut top as illustrated roll out a sheet $\frac{1}{2}$ inch thick of the same clay as the pot, allow it to stiffen, and then cut to the appropriate size and fasten together with slip.

ADDING THE FITTINGS

There are a number of push-in fittings on the market. Some utilize cork strip, others plastic flanges. None is very secure if a large shade is used. The alternatives are either to cement a threaded tube into the neck using epoxy or one of the tile cements or, better still, to use the type of fitting (Illustration 55) which is very firm and secure and has the added advantage that it can be easily dismantled and used on another base if required.

These fittings necessitate access to the inside of the lamp base, and it is essential to cut away the base for this purpose (Illustration 56). A small-bladed penknife will do this quite neatly.

Put a nut and washer on one end of the threaded tube and insert it through the neck from the inside of the pot. If you can get your hand inside, this will be simple, otherwise use a length of wood or dowelling with the threaded fitting wedged on. Drop another washer over the top and screw the second nut down until it is reasonably tight. It is possible to dispense with the top nut by screwing the switched lamp holder straight onto the rod. With this type of fitting, the flex will be threaded into the pot. Do not forget to drill a small hole near the bottom to bring it out again.

One additional note: check the fittings on the leather-hard base, and make allowance for

Illustration 55. Lamp fittings to complete the ceramic lamp base.

43

Illustration 56. How to cut open the base of the lamp to permit insertion of the screw-in lamp fittings.

Illustration 57. Carving the lamp base with a wooden modeling tool.

shrinkage in firing. Then remove the fittings so that the base may be biscuited, glazed and fired. When the base has been completed, then put the fittings into place permanently.

FINISHING AND DECORATING

A carved surface makes for an attractive lamp base. The light will throw interesting shadows and, if it can be fired to stoneware temperature, little or no glazing is needed. A sponge dipped in a darkish glaze and simply rubbed into the surface will suffice. The carved line can be filled or, with careful sponging, left blank as a contrast. Spinning with copper or iron, using a coarse brush, will again emphasize the decoration and give a varied and fresh finish. Do not dab with the brush or try to follow the cut line too precisely, but use swift strokes which will complement and not confuse the carving.

Various tools can be used for cutting the clay, from a wooden modeling tool to a fine knife or comb. In any case, aim at boldness and freedom of movement and of design. The clay will cut most crisply when it is leather-hard.

There are many possible variations in style, stroke, and pattern. Experiment on a spare piece of clay before you start on your pot. The weathering of rocks, tree bark, architectural columns are a few design sources you can utilize.

Illustration 58
A completed stoneware lamp base by Evelyn Ross.

6. Pottery Dishes without Molds

Many problems are associated with the use of plaster-of-Paris molds in a small workshop or classroom. Plaster is something of a hazard, for even the smallest piece of plaster falling into the clay will lead to bloating, cracking, or even to an explosion in the kiln. Secondly, plaster molds are bulky to store. Consequently, a knowledge of other methods of producing "molded" dishes and pots without the use of plaster molds is invaluable to the potter.

The easiest method of producing dishes of individual shape and size without molds is to design the form, cut a template from stiff paper, and following the template to cut out the shape of the dish from a sheet of clay. As with all techniques, this method demands a little practice, but you can soon become proficient at it and enjoy making dishes of your own design.

The method of making dishes without molds has its limitations. Dishes formed in this fashion look their best when fairly chunky in style, made from grogged clay, and stoneware fired. Plaster-molded dishes, on the other hand, are most suitable for slip decoration and glazing with tin glazes; ideally, these should be formed of earthenware clays and suitably glazed.

The advantages of forming without molds are that little or no equipment is needed, and that an infinite variety of shapes and sizes can be made simply by means of templates cut from paper.

Illustration 59
Large stoneware dish (13 inches across) decorated with red slip and a dolomite glaze, fired in an electric kiln at 2282° F. (1250° C.). Dish by Trudi Moos.

Illustration 60. How to cut the template.

MAKING A RECTANGULAR DISH

The set of illustrations (60 through 73) shows the significant stages in the making of a rectangular dish with this method. The steps are as follows:

1. Form the template. Draw the precise shape and size of your dish (plus allowance for shrinkage) on a piece of stiff paper and cut it out. For a regular and even shape, fold the paper into four and cut as shown in Illustration 60. This works only for squares and rectangles, of course.

2. Roll out a sheet of clay evenly and carefully on a rolling cloth, using guide sticks for thickness control. For most dishes, $\frac{3}{8}$ to $\frac{1}{2}$ inch thickness is recommended.

3. Place the paper template on the clay and cut out the general shape with a spatula tool or potter's knife. Cut with the tool in an upright position. This is easier to do if you turn the clay

Illustration 61. Typical templates for triangular, square, and rectangular dishes.

47

Illustration 62. How to roll out the sheet of clay with use of guide sticks. Start at middle and, using even pressure with both hands, roll out toward edges.

around as the work proceeds so that you are always cutting toward yourself.

4. Next make a special cut at the corners, holding the tool at an angle (see Illustration 64). It does not matter which way the cut slopes so long as both sides slope the same way. At this stage transfer the clay slab from the cloth on which it was rolled to a more easily trans-

portable and porous surface such as a modeling board.

5. Coat each face of the angle with thick slip of the clay body and bring the two sides together, as in Illustrations 65 and 66. Illustration 66 shows the outside view of Illustration 65, indicating the overlapping resulting from the angled cut. This makes the join much stronger

Illustration 63. How to cut the general shape of the template from the rolled-out clay.

48

Illustration 64
How to cut the corners on an angle: both sides
slope the same way for ease in joining.

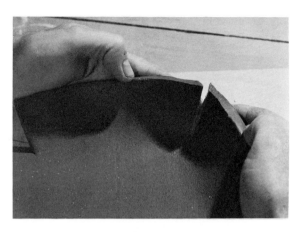

Illustration 65
Each face of the corner angle is coated with slip;
the sides are brought together and joined.

Illustration 66
Outside view of slit join and resulting overlap of
the angled cut.

Illustration 67
Support sides of the dish with the palms of your
hands while joining corners.

Illustration 68
Larger dishes require additional support during the
drying process. Triangular coils of clay work well.

Illustration 69
Smooth the inside of the dish with a rubber kidney
while the clay is still soft and pliable.

49

Illustration 70. Even the rim off while the clay is still soft, or trim when leather-hard.

and easier to work together. Lap the edges over well so that the join can be smoothed out without thinning the clay wall.

6. In working across the corners, support the sides with the palms of your hands as in Illustration 67, lifting the corners while the clay is still soft. If the clay stiffens, cracks may develop underneath. The walls of small dishes will stand their own weight, but those of larger pieces need some support. Use large coils beaten to a triangular section, as shown in Illustration 68. These will do the job effectively and retain the contour of the walls.

7. While the clay is still fairly soft, the inside of the dish can be smoothed over with a rubber kidney (Illustration 69) while your hand

Illustration 71. Trim and smooth the inside of the dish with a steel kidney.

50

Illustration 72. Smooth the outside of the dish with a tool.

supports the dish. The tool will gently round out the form.

8. When the dish has stiffened somewhat, level the top edge. Push a needle awl through a piece of stiff cardboard at the required height and angle for the cut and draw it around the rim of the dish as shown in Illustration 70.

Another method of leveling the rim is to leave the dish uneven at this stage and then to plane or cut the rim when the dish is leather-hard.

9. When the dish has dried to leather-hard and is too stiff to be deformed, a final trimming and smoothing of the inside with a steel kidney is recommended (Illustration 71).

Illustration 73. Finish rim with a pie-crust design.

10. The top edge of the dish can be finished in various ways: planed flat, angled, or rounded. A traditional and attractive rim is the "pie-crust" rim, achieved by the repetition of regular indentations with a tool as in Illustration 73. This is a decorative detail which contrasts well with the plain face of the dish and strengthens the rim by compression.

11. Finally the outside can be smoothed over with a tool or planed. Rest the dishes on their rims to dry. In this way the air will reach the base and the dish will dry more evenly.

Any style of decoration may be used: resist, brushwork, slip, etc. though, for stoneware, the dishes often have sufficient character for the exterior to be left plain and the inside covered with an interesting glaze.

Before biscuiting, make certain that the base is flat and that the dishes stand on a flat shelf in the kiln.

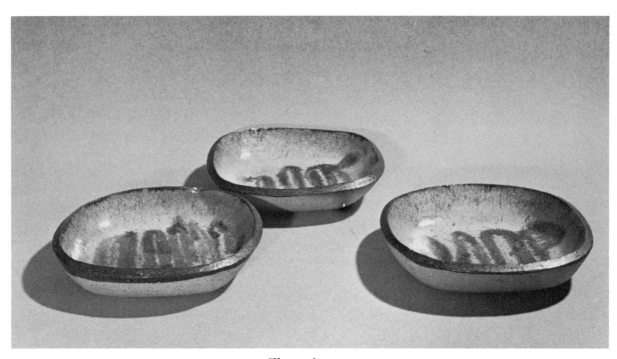

Illustration 74
Three similar-sized dishes made from a single template, glazed on the inside only, with rims and design brushed in with manganese.

7. Handles

Illustration 75. Hanging pot with lugs by Bernard Rooke.

The forerunner of the handle was the pierced lug, one on either side of a pot, through which string, or its equivalent, was threaded in order to suspend the pot in an open doorway where it hung and swung, keeping its contents cool by evaporation.

Such lugs are found on the magnificent Shang Yin pots from Central China and on ceramics from most near-tropical countries

from Africa to Peru. Bottles, designed to be suspended from a horseman's saddle by leather thongs persisted throughout the world into quite modern times. In fact, lugs are still used by potters, sometimes decoratively or for practical purposes where the pot is designed to be suspended (see Illustration 75). A new range of forms is possible with this type of pot as it needs no flat base.

But the true handle is used for lifting a pot to drink or pour, or when the pot itself is hot from cooking. Handles, consequently, belong on pots only if they can be used in a practical way. A handle can and should add grace, strength, and interest to a pot, but it must be an integral part of it. A handle will balance the lip or spout; it will invite the hand or finger to close around it. The handle is not particularly effective in completing a curve in the manner of Greek pottery, for if one moves to one side of the profile view, the curve alters and breaks.

Illustration 76
Porcelain teapot with separately molded handle.
Berlin factory, about 1775.

53

THE GREAT VARIETY OF HANDLES

The type of handle applied to commercial pottery differs from that found on the craftsman potter's work. In industry, the handle may be carefully considered in relation to the pot, but it is always made in a press or slip-mold as a separate entity. A distinct point of junction is thus apparent in the commercial handle (Illustration 76). Note the "stop" or thumb-hold at the top, which has been worked into the design to prevent the hand from slipping. Commercially produced handles need not have the smooth, arched flow of the pulled handle but may be angled or built up from broken curves—a freedom which has led to some notable excesses. The clean articulation of parts is distinctive of the best industrial ceramics.

At the other end of the scale is the hand-crafted English medieval jug, where the handle springs like a branch from the main form to which it is firmly secured by strokes of the thumb (Illustration 77). This apparently natural growth of the handle is satisfying from all angles, not merely from a profile view. The strong pulling lines and bold wipe of the clay on each side of the juncture are delights in themselves. This thumb movement at once fastens the handle and decorates the pot.

Illustration 77
Medieval earthenware jug with strong, pulled handle. English. Green galena glaze over shoulder.

Illustration 78
Contemporary stoneware cream pitcher with pulled handle. The space between the handle and the body forms a D-shape.

PLACEMENT

The placing of a handle is governed by three main considerations:

- The curves of the main form.
- The number of fingers required to lift the vessel when full of liquid. The thickness and width of the handle in direct relation to this weight.
- Physical and formal balance.

Between the curve of the pot and that of the handle, there is a space. Not only must this be sufficient to accommodate the finger or fingers comfortably, but the shape of the space is of great esthetic importance. On a more or less cylindrical jug or beaker it may be no more than the simple letter D. The one-finger handle in Illustration 78 is an example. On the inward curve between the belly and neck of a well-designed jug, this space will be very subtle. The jug in Illustration 79 shows these related curves merging into a whole which resembles an airfoil.

Illustration 79
Details of stoneware jug handle with flattened curve to provide grip and balance and to match the shoulder of the pot. By Geoffrey Whiting.

It is usually advisable to spring the handle across a concave section of the pot form. If the handle straddles a bulge, a rather ugly crescent is formed and the handle may become awkwardly long, difficult to hold, or both.

The question of placing handles high or low is a matter of some controversy. As a general rule, however, a handle which springs higher than the rim of the pot will make it awkward to invert for draining, while one that is too near the base will not allow a firm grip when picking the pot up or setting it down.

Within these limits, however, a case can be made for both positions. For instance, the center of gravity of a beaker may be said to be below the half-way mark since it is rarely full of liquid. A low handle should, therefore, give a better balance. On the other hand, the leverage resulting from a low placing gives less control when the rim approaches the lips. Placement is a matter for individual discretion.

The common salt-glazed bottle often had a very high handle. The position was due partly to the fact that it was used for carrying rather than for tipping the bottle, and partly to the high shoulder on an otherwise cylindrical form. This handle was made for hard wear. It was thick and well joined and yet still retained a strong and lively character. The vigor of this type of handle came from the speed with which it was, of necessity, made and applied. Slow, fussy work will rarely give satisfactory results.

TEAPOTS

The side handle on teapots is the accepted and most common style. It has, in fact, some disadvantages. First, the leverage is considerable when the teapot is heavy with liquid; second, on a flattish shape it results in a squat overall form; third, it is always difficult to spring a handle around a full curve. To some extent, therefore, the side placement controls the main pot form.

One alternative is to spring the handle over the lid. The cane handle with two lugs is now fairly familiar in the West through the Eastern influence, which has been dominant among craftsman potters since the 1920's. The principle may be taken a stage further with a

Illustration 80
Teapot with ceramic handle sprung over lid. By Sheila Fournier.

55

pottery handle instead of a cane one. For this, however, you must be fairly adept at pulling a long handle and curving it over at the right moment if it is not to sag or break.

CASSEROLES

Simple lugs are often sufficient for gripping and lifting a hot casserole, but many prefer a side handle, especially on soup bowls and poaching dishes. The side lug may be thrown hollow, tapering toward the pot, or slightly bulbous at the holding end, or it may be pulled. The pulled lug can be made separately and attached when leather-hard, or pulled direct from a wedge of clay on the body of the bowl. A simple, attractive and lively pulled handle appears on the Leach Pottery poaching dish in Illustration 81.

MAIN PRINCIPLES

To sum up, here are the main principles for making good handles.

• The first essential is for you to consider the handle and its style of placing as part of the whole design and not as a problem to be faced after the main form has been completed.

• Second, it is not possible to separate the practical and esthetic values of the handle and the main form. One springs from, and conditions, the other.

• Finally, try to see the difference between a strong and a weak handle and to analyze where the weakness lies, whether it is in inadequate size, flabby curve, bad placement, or poor joining.

PULLING A HANDLE

Although the word "pulling" is always used in describing the making of pottery handles, it is, in fact, a misnomer. As in all pottery techniques, the action is that of squeezing the clay; the extension of the handle as this is being done gives the impression it is being pulled out.

Illustration 82 shows the positions of the thumb and forefinger in the action of forming a handle. The finger is moved progressively down behind the thumb as the hand slides down the clay so that the opening contracts in the manner of a camera diaphragm. In this way, a handle is formed which tapers toward the lower end.

Illustration 81. Poaching dish with pulled side handle. Leach Pottery.

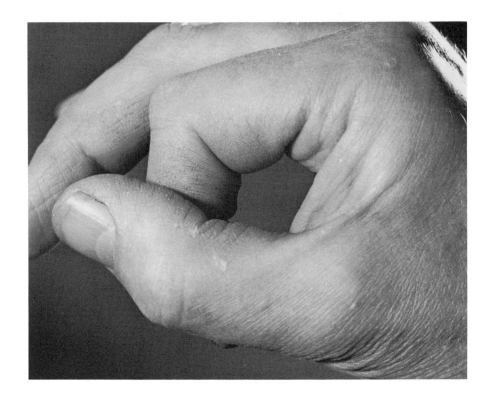

Illustration 82. The positions of the thumb and forefinger in the action of pulling a handle.

To start, take a well-wedged piece of clay of about one pound in weight and roll it to the shape of a blunt cone. Hold the cone by the large end and dip the thinner end in water. Wet the other hand and, holding the finger and thumb as illustrated, stroke and squeeze the tail in a series of steady downward movements.

If the handle becomes thin or cracks any-where along its length, nip it off and pull some more clay from the base of the cone. Any sudden change of pressure (or bubbles or bad wedging) will spoil the handle.

Make certain the clay is continuously wet. The clay consistency should be similar to that used for throwing. It may help to "pull" the clay over in a curve rather than straight down.

The final shaping of the section can be produced through various finger positions. An example is shown in Illustration 84 where the clay lies in the crook of the first finger, which flattens and shapes the back, while the thumb impresses a slightly concave form to the face. Finger and thumb together on the face will give a central rib, but the method outlined above will give a comfortable and satisfactory shape.

Illustration 83
Pulling the handle in a tapering fashion down from the cone.

57

The handle can now be placed on a board after being cut from the wedge of clay from which it was pulled. Cut the handle at the point where it really begins to thicken out. The type of board is important. Wood or plaster is adequate. Asbestos cement is not so good; plastic or metal surfaces are quite unsatisfactory. By drying the handle as suggested in Illustration 85 (rather than by hanging it straight down, as is common practice) it is not so likely to break when bent to shape on the pot. The handle can be applied with the clay in a firmer condition, and the completed handle is less liable to crack or spring away while drying.

Illustration 85
Pulled and cut handles laid out to dry on a board. Drying handles in this position helps to avoid cracking and springing from the pot.

APPLYING THE HANDLE

The handle is ready to fix to the pot when it has dried to the point where it is still possible to bend or straighten it without sign of cracking, yet is sufficiently firm to hold without marking or distorting. It should not sag out of shape when it has been fixed to the pot.

Cut the handle at the point where it begins to thicken appreciably. The sense of integration between pot and handle which is so essential is largely dependent on this upper termination. If the cut is made too far down the handle the section will be too narrow to provide a strong butted join.

Cut the handle where it will be, or will appear to be, strong enough to make a good join. Trim it to a hollow curve. Try it against the pot and cut roughly to length. The angle of cut (as seen from the side) will, of course, determine the angle at which it will spring from the pot—upwards, downwards, or straight out—and this will greatly affect its style and character.

Score the pot where the join is to be made. Brush the appropriate slip onto the handle and a little onto the pot. The curved cut should flatten a little as the join is pressed home, and the clay thus pushed out on either side can be used to weld the handle on more firmly. The foregoing points are clearly shown in Illustration 86. Take care not to squeeze the handle during this operation. Hold it firmly with your thumb above and a crooked first finger beneath.

The handle must now be curved over to the appropriate shape and size and cut to length. Score. Brush lower junction with slip and press the base firmly home as in Illustration 87.

Alternatively, the handle can be cut to the appropriate angle to butt at the base as well as at the top. Simply press it to the pot—with a dab of slip. This is a useful termination for cup handles and other small pots.

THROWN HANDLES

Handles can be made on the wheel for casseroles, soup bowls, side-handled coffee pots, etc. Such a handle, thrown in the manner of a small pot, is shown in Illustration 88. The form may be bulbous, as shown, or slightly flaring at the top. It should be hollow almost down to the wheelhead. Although this example

59

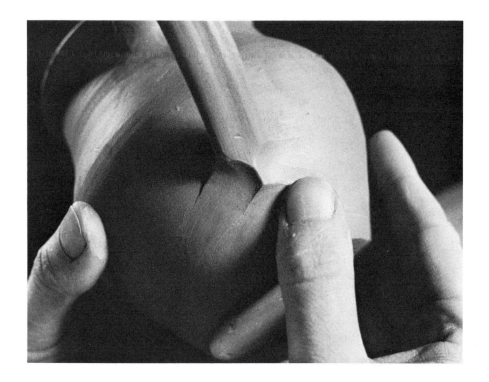

is being thrown from a small piece of clay, a more practical method is to center a larger piece and then throw several handles from it in succession.

The handle is cut from the wheel; allow it to dry until it reaches a leather-hard state similar to that of the bowl to which it is to be joined. It is then trimmed to fit snugly, and fastened on by scoring with slip. Be sure that there is sufficient room under the handle for your fingers to grip it without tipping the bowl.

The virtues of a first-class handle are demonstrated in the fine teapot by Geoffrey Whiting shown in Illustration 90. The subtle and lively shape gives an easy grip and good balance. Note the slight straightening of the top and back of the curve, which leaves ample room for the fingers without springing too far from the shoulder of the pot, the form of which it reflects but does not exactly repeat. The rim of the pot is left intact and uninterrupted. Finally, there is the "stop" at the top of the handle which adds interest for the eye and has a very practical value.

Illustration 88
Side handle being thrown on the wheel. The handle is in the form of a hollow lug.

Illustration 89
Handle in leather-hard state is luted onto the pot.

Illustration 90. Teapot
with slightly
straightened handle and
stop at the top. By
Geoffrey Whiting.

8. Slipware

Slip decoration is fundamental to pottery and covers a very wide field: from primitive scrawls to the Greek virtuosity of line; from 18th-century bucolic humor to the cold precision of modern industrial tableware. It is often difficult to distinguish between a slip and a pigment, but generally slip refers to either natural liquid clay or a mixture with a high clay content.

In early decoration on Susa and Mesopotamian pots and many other early pots, the slip was laid on with a brush or its equivalent. It is the commonest of all early techniques, but is rarely seen on later pieces. This is because the brushwork gave a thin and uneven coating which was adequate and long-lasting when the pot was left as biscuit, but proved insufficient as soon as glaze was applied.

To test this on an earthenware clay, try brushing buff slip on red clay or vice-versa and later glazing with a normal lead glaze. The slip will probably disappear entirely. The glaze, in melting, uses a thin layer of the pot surface to fulfill its glass-making function and so the thin coating of slip is turned into virtually clear glass. To attain a layer of slip thick enough to glaze, either flood the surface of the dish or pot with slip, trail it on, or build up the thickness by using a very heavily loaded brush or by repeated applications. A rather static and labored style of built-up strokes was used industrially in the 19th century and was called "paté-sur-paté." Where a loaded brush is lifted from the clay surface and at the perimeter of a stroke, the slip tends to pile up and is more likely to remain effective under a glaze.

But must you use glaze? The clean, almost mint condition of many pots 2,000 or 3,000 years old indicates that discoloration is not necessarily a factor. There are several alternatives to, or precursors of, true glazed, i.e., glass-covered, pottery.

BURNISHING

The simplest and perhaps the earliest method of finishing pottery was to burnish with a smooth-surfaced tool, a pebble or a bone. Today the back of a spoon is a useful burnisher. Burnishing can be assisted by a coating of hematite—a fine grain clay-bearing iron oxide—which will also color the surface. The work must be done when the clay is leather-hard. For sawdust and other simple or primitive firings, ferric oxide is a very suitable finish, giving a lustrous black in reduction firing and a red-brown in an oxidation firing up to about 1742° F. (950° C.). At 1832° F. (1000° C.) and over, the color dies somewhat.

VARNISHING AND POLISHING

The application of non-ceramic finishes is frowned upon today. They can lead to degenerate work and miss the true excitement of ceramics—alteration through fire.

Nevertheless, ancient American pots had some such surface treatment which is bright and intact after some hundreds of years. Of course, the clay itself *must* be fired to red heat at least if it is to warrant the description of "ceramic." Quite temporary finishes have been applied to biscuit, and one can find traces of raw pigment on pots and figures from such sophisticated periods as the T'ang dynasty in China. In Africa, pots, while still very hot from the fire, are beaten with a local plant, and the sap burns onto the surface, or they are "given a quick bath in a decoction made from the pods of locust beans," which results in a bright black polish. A recent book recommends soaking higher-fired ware in milk, leaving it for a week to sour and dry before washing off. Another suggestion is to use clear acrylic paint, leaving the ware to soak and then washing it clean.

Illustration 91
Slip decoration.

Illustration 92

Pottery-making, Greece's oldest art, began about 900 B.C. At first the designs were mathematical and abstract, but gradually became more realistic. Many vase paintings represent scenes from everyday life or mythology.

LEVIGATED SLIP

The terra sigillata of the Greeks and Romans was a levigated slip which utilized only the finest clay particles, possibly with some form of soda or potash to deflocculate, and gave the gloss on "samian" and on red-and-black figure vases. Although rarely used again, it was the standard finish on high-class pottery for 1500 years.

VITRIFICATION OF CLAY AND SLIP

The temperature at which the clay body and slip vitrify (that is, harden), tighten and turn to glass, will vary according to the clay used and the metal oxide content of the slip. Vitrification was not common on early pots because of the primitive nature of the firing. Today, almost all clays are fired to maturity and the vitrification of clay and slip is useful for tiles, garden and sculptural pieces, and for slip effects which would be spoiled by glaze. Porosity, and thus discoloration and frost damage, are eliminated.

The wide range of decoration possible with slip can be gauged by comparing, for instance, the Greek vase painting and sgraffito of the "Golden Age"—highly sophisticated, taut and compelling on an intellectual level although emotionally cold—with the freely decorated Persian Samarkand and Sari wares, sometimes naive but wholly satisfying. Between two such extremes is the pre-Columbian pot decoration from Aztec and Maya peoples, precisely and skillfully drawn and charged with a sense of ritual and, sometimes, menace.

The slip palette is quite extensive: primitive red on buff; Greek terracotta; white and black; red, orange-red, and purple from America; sage green and light red from Persia.

Earlier potters did not make the distinction between slip and glaze made today. They would seek out and use "earths" high in metallic oxide content such as ochres. Many a very impure garden clay will give bright iron colors on biscuit even when fired as high as 2282° F. (1250° C.). The modern practice of staining slips with oxides never quite achieves the same quality.

In general, the higher color-content mixtures are used for painting, spinning, and applications which result in a thinner coating. They are used also for special glazing techniques as under tin glaze. The clay in a slip has the double effect of diluting the color and also of spreading it evenly over the surface, a result impossible to obtain with plain pigment. Many "self-color" industrial wares are slip coated. A "loaded" or high-pigment slip would probably approximate more nearly the materials used on ancient painted pots than the standard stained slips normally used today.

Another important, although less dramatic, use of slip has been to whiten and refine the surface of pottery. At a technically more advanced level, shards of Turkish Isnik plates show that the body was comparatively coarse and that the "ground" for the painting was a thin, white layer laid onto the surface in the manner of a slip, and the whole covered with a clear glaze.

The advent of glaze led to other styles of slipware. There are examples of buff slip roughly brushed onto medieval pots. By the

64

17th century, glaze had, in the West, come into general use and slip decoration concentrated on trailing and sgraffito, techniques which involve a thicker coating which will resist the effects of the clay-hungry glaze. The large platters, loving cups, and other commemorative pieces decorated in this way are familiar to most potters. There is a fascinating continuity between the 10th-century Persian dishes and English village slipwares in the use of a dotted line, often white dots on a black line.

With simple trailing it is difficult to avoid linear effect, especially on the dry background as was used in the "Toft" and other dishes. In these designs, however, there are considerable areas filled in with contrasting slips, but little research has been made into the methods used. The color was usually solid and opaque and a substantial coating must have been applied.

On wet grounds, and where the trailing is done immediately after flooding the surface, a wider line is possible, while feathering also can give a certain solidity. On many of the small cups of the late 17th century, potters performed the not inconsiderable feat of feathering the lower half, closely trailed lines being drawn with a quill into a marbled effect. This was combined with lettering in slip—such inscriptions as "No Pope" or "The best is not too good for you."

A very thin slip will also produce a wider line, but it is difficult to control. Of the many slip techniques the most direct and satisfying is the trailing of slip onto a liquid ground. The typical stages in three applications of this technique are: running slip, free trailing and trailing on a blocked-out area, and trailing and feathering.

Feathering was commonest in the late 18th and the 19th century English village slipwares, and has been revived now by individual studio potters.

The ideal is to achieve an appearance of liquid, flowing slip even in the finished fired and glazed piece. The style requires very little equipment apart from the trailer or "tracer." This is a slip container, conveniently small and light, with a small orifice and some means of controlling the flow of slip from it. It has taken a variety of ingenious forms. A simple, early

tracer was a biscuited "bulb" fitted with a hollow quill and controlled by means of a hole in the top, over which the thumb was placed. By relaxing the pressure of the thumb, air was allowed to enter the bulb and the slip flowed out through the quill. You can make a tracer out of a triangular piece of waxed paper or soft plastic, folding it into the form of an old-fashioned candy or sugar bag.

The commonest types of trailers on the commercial market consist of rubber bags with glass or plastic nozzles. The stiff rubber bulb type can be filled with slip of a reasonable thickness by suction, and this is an advantage.

Other rubber tracers on the market have soft bags which must be filled through a funnel. The nozzles are awkward to insert (dry fingers make the job much easier), but slip control is possible through both pressure and gravity and the process is quite sensitive and delicate. Other types include baby's bottles, and glass and rubber tubes.

Illustration 93
An example of pre-Columbian earthenware decoration.

Illustration 94. Slip being trailed in "blots." Work quickly—the trailing must be applied immediately after background slip is poured on.

Illustration 95. The "blots" must decrease from top to bottom. The dish must be held firmly and the slip shaken sharply downward.

Illustration 96. Very attractive designs result, as this dish by John Shelley proves.

Illustration 97. Here the slip has been shaken into the middle of the bowl and then given a sharp twist.

Illustration 98. Free trailing on a blocked-out area. A sponge is used to wipe away an area of the background slip.

Illustration 99. The area wiped away is filled with a contrasting slip poured from a spoon. It could also be trailed in.

Illustration 100. First stage in trailing of a crab design.

Illustration 101. Next stage in the trailing of the crab using red and buff slips.

Illustration 102. Trailing and feathering being done on a flat slab of rolled-out clay with a soft bag of trailer.

Illustration 103. Here a quill with the feathers stripped off is used.

Illustration 104. A close-up of a late 18th-century trailed and feathered dish.

Illustration 105. A combination of trailing and run slip by June Smith. Lines were trailed across the dish, extra slip was fed into top left and bottom right and the dish tilted both ways.

69

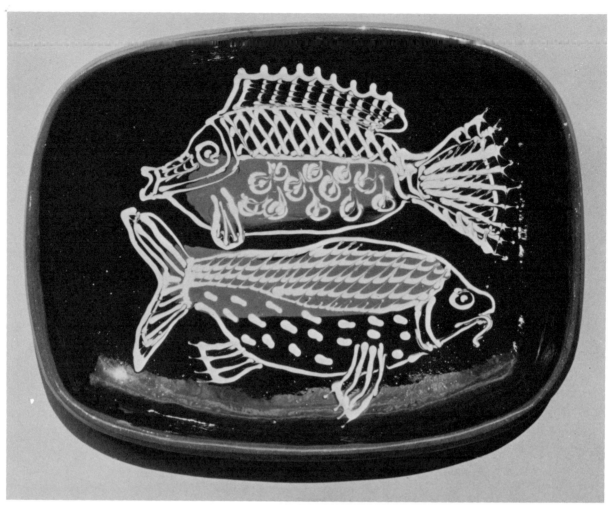

Illustration 106

A slip-trailed dish covered with honey glaze by Pam Fitzgerald. Slip was applied thickly and quickly to leather-hard dish, fixed in biscuit firing, glazed, and fired to maturity.

APPLYING SLIP TO DISHES

Thrown and molded dishes are suitable for running slip, free trailing or trailing on a blocked-out area, but feathering is best done on the flat clay and the dish made over a hump mold as soon as the decorated surface is sufficiently dry.

Feathering demands care and watchfulness that the body of the dish does not get too dry to take the form of the mold, which should have a fairly shallow and even curve. It *is* possible to ease the slab of clay into a hollow mold after feathering, but this demands practice and great care and, again, the clay must be in just the right (not quite leather-hard) state.

Wet newspaper laid under the sheet of clay, with the edges damped occasionally, will help.

For the other forms of slipware, work is done on the leather-hard dish. Remove it from the mold to flood on the background slip. This makes the job cleaner and more controllable, and slip will not spill over the mold. The slip-covered dish can be dropped back into the mold for support during trailing. A thrown dish or bowl does not generally need support if it is designed with an appreciation of the stresses inherent in slipwork in mind.

To dry molded dishes without deformation of the rim, reverse onto a sheet of plywood quite soon after the decoration has been done. Lay the board on top of the mold and turn the whole thing over. The mold can then be lifted from the dish.

For free trailing, use a dish large enough, say 9 to 14 inches in diameter, to allow for broad and easy sweeps with the trailer. It is essentially a rapid and lively technique. For the trailed line to sink into the background slip, the dish must be freshly coated and still fluid. Before starting work, have the trailers full and everything ready—including an idea of your basic design. This will almost certainly undergo modification as the work progresses.

As a general rule, the thinner the slip, the quicker you must work and the livelier will be the result. Thick slip, which needs some force to push it through the trailer nozzle, will lie on the surface and give a less fluent and integrated line. Control comes only with practice and beginners are advised to use a fairly creamy slip, but to bear in mind that the ideal slip is thinner and the movement more spontaneous.

Before stirring slip please remember the golden rule—pour off the clear water first. If, after stirring, it is then too thick just add more water. If the slip is too thin, there is no quick remedy. You can: add more powdered clay if the slip is a buff or red one; add appropriate proportions of clay and pigment to a colored slip, which is tantamount to making up a new batch; or put the work off to another day when the slip will have settled and the excess liquid can be poured off. In any case, sieve the amount of slip you need to use—even if it has been sieved quite recently. Dried or even slightly thicker particles of slip will spoil the effect of liquid flow on which good slipware quality depends.

SOME SLIP FORMULAS

Four or five slips are sufficient for slip-trailing—the simplest combination of red, buff, and black for true and dramatic slipwares.

It is the work, the design, the balance, and the spontaneity which are of paramount importance, not a large batch of colors. Five basic slips and their ingredients are:

1. Buff slip. 100% buff clay.
2. Red slip. 100% red clay.
3. Black slip. 100 grams red clay plus—
       9% manganese oxide
     or 4% iron oxide
       6% manganese oxide
       1% cobalt oxide
4. Green slip. 100 grams buff clay plus—
       1.25% copper oxide
       1.25% chrome oxide
5. Blue slip. 100 grams buff clay plus—
       1% cobalt oxide
       1% manganese oxide

There are almost as many recipes for slips as for glazes, with additions to whiten, to vitrify, to assist adhesion to the body, to "break" the colors, and so on, but the old traditional potters would have had none of these refinements.

The use of the clay body as far as possible for your slips, plus the use of slips on barely leather-hard clay dishes, will usually give satisfactory results.

9. Glazes

Illustration 107

Morning coffee service, glazed and fired to stoneware—2282° F. (1250° C.). Note that all forms were thrown at the wheel and cylinders were finished with low-set pulled handles.

A fascination with glazes can become an end in itself, but this does not make for good potting. Nevertheless, an original and attractive finish can add greatly to a pot. Much is missed in ceramic glazes (many new glazes are available) through indifferent and careless testing which can mislead rather than reveal. The subject is an intricate one and the following are just a few guidelines.

The first thing to realize is that there is no such thing as a recipe for a glaze in the sense that a fixed result will be obtained. The "recipe," though a major factor, is only one of many. The variations are more pronounced in stoneware than in earthenware. To take an example from recent experience: a gray-green earthenware glaze of no great merit which had lain unused for a long while suddenly became a great favorite. It developed a new richness and depth of color because it was tried on a red clay rather than on buff.

Apart from the obvious factors of recipe and firing temperature, the following factors dominate the behavior of a glaze: kiln size, clay body, speed of firing and cooling, thickness of glaze application, and the position of the piece in the glaze kiln. In addition, glaze results also depend on the inevitable variations in raw materials and the fact that glaze alters slightly as one uses it, generally getting a little harder towards the end of the batch.

You may be surprised that kiln size affects the fired glaze results, but this is particularly the case in stoneware. Speed of firing is, of course, often allied to kiln size. There is little resemblance between the fired results of the same batch of glaze when fired in (a) a small test kiln, (b) a slowish front-opening 5 cubic foot kiln and (c) a similar-sized but quick-firing top-loader.

Sometimes the most attractive results come from the tiny kiln and the least lively from the slower large one. There are many virtues of quick firing followed by rapid cooling to 1652° F. (900° C.) for many stoneware glazes. It is well known that quick cooling to the comparatively inert conditions at 1472–1652° F. (800–900° C.) will assist the formation of glassy materials by inhibiting crystal growth. This will often give a brightness to an otherwise rather dull surfaced glaze.

A glaze test, which at first seems a failure, may on close inspection be much more promising where the glaze is markedly thicker or thinner. An extreme example of this occurred some time ago. An earthenware glaze which should have been transparent failed to melt at all at 1976° F. (1080° C.). Tried in a stoneware kiln, it bubbled wildly and was written off. A later study of the test, however, showed a curious effect where the glaze was very thin and new trials, lightly dabbed on with a sponge, gave highly original results—varied and sometimes greenish, eroded surfaces very useful for large coiled pots in grogged clay.

TEST RECORDS

It is virtually impossible to record all the factors which influence a glaze test result, but the mere note of recipe and temperature is not very useful. Obviously, you will have to make your own decision on the information which will be of most use to you, but the following important topics are recommended as headings on your test notes:

1. TEST NUMBER. A simple running number is advised. Codes can get bogged down.

2. RECIPE. Preferably given in percentages for easier comparison, also total amount by gram weight.

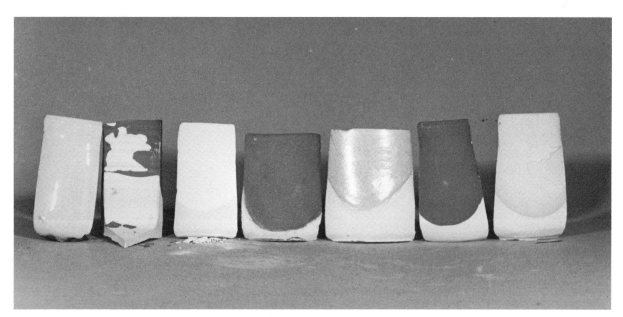

Illustration 108

Seven test pots and shards glazed and numbered. Write all major facts in test records, and number them as on test pot for easy identification after firing.

73

Illustration 109
For glaze tests, throw quick repetition bowls from "the hump" of a centered 3- or 4-pound ball of clay.

3. Test Piece. Note whether a thrown bowl or cylinder, or a tile. Note if tile was tilted or flat.

4. Body. Color or clay mix, rough or smooth.

5. Glaze Thickness.

6. Test Surface. Plain or engraved.

7. Position in Kiln. Roughly given as floor, top or center.

8. Kiln and Firing. Temperature. Record if kiln was fired especially fast or slow.

In recording your glaze test results, list the color, type of surface, transparency or opacity and other notes of interest, alterations which seem called for, plus a general assessment of the success or attractiveness of the result. A provisional description or name is useful for the glaze, as it is difficult to discuss an anonymous glaze.

It is more practicable to write this information in what might be called horizontal columns, i.e., across the page of a glaze record book or across a file card. You may not have the patience or time to fill in all columns for

every test, but this is well worthwhile and will save time in the long run.

TEMPERATURE

Standardizing of procedure is advised in keeping records of glaze firings. With a pyrometer on your electric kiln this is simple. The temperature shown may not be the true temperature, but it will be fairly constant. With a cone, some easily recognizable stage in its fall should be established.

One system is to note the precise moment when the tip of the cone to which the kiln is being fired touches the shelf, and then to time the firing in minutes afterwards, e.g., 7 cone, 8 minutes. To achieve accuracy the same type of cone socket is always used, as this controls the fall. With oxidized stoneware, minutes matter at top heat.

GLAZE THICKNESS

Always the most tricky part of glaze testing is to establish the thickness of the applied glaze. On a test piece one can scratch through to

Illustration 110
Cut test bowls from hump with a needle or wire.

74

judge thickness. A regular biscuit temperature helps. Industrially, and in some more scientifically-minded potteries, a hydrometer is used to test the consistency of glaze in the bin. This can be purchased, or may be simply a piece of wood or a test tube so weighted at one end that it floats upright and is about two-thirds submerged in water. This level is marked on the hydrometer and a series of numbered intervals painted or scratched below this line. In a glaze it will stand higher out of the liquid according to its thickness. Make a note of the new level and record it so that a similar glaze consistency can be achieved each time.

TEST PIECES

Your test pieces can take various forms, but the odd bit of broken biscuit so often used is the least satisfactory. Instead use: curved tiles about 3 inches × 1 inch × $\frac{1}{4}$ inch cut from a thrown cylinder or rolled out and dried over a rolling pin; circular discs about 2 inches across with a hole in them, strung together like Chinese coins or tied to the glaze batch they represent; small bowls or cylinders; or full-size production pieces.

Use the pieces in this order: first trials on curved tiles and, if rewarding, on bowls and cylinders with the discs as records. (See Illustration 108.)

LABELING AND GRADING TESTS

Labeling and marking are vitally important and often neglected aspects of glaze testing. Assume that you will *never* be able to remember what a test piece represented and always mark it or number it clearly in a ceramic pigment. A cobalt-manganese mixture is clear and reliable in oxidation. Then label the glaze itself with a tie-on or stick on a label with as much information or code to information as possible.

About 300 grams is the minimum batch for a reliable test using accurate scales.

When a definite series of tests is to be made, it is not necessary to make up a fresh glaze batch each time. Two batches, one at each extreme of the series can be tried, e.g., a clear glaze and one with 10% of pigment. Mix as follows, using a standard consistency of glaze

Illustration 111

A stoneware lamp base or candle holder made by slab work, utilizing different glazes inside and out.

and a standard measure—a spoon or a small bowl.

1st SERIES

To 5 parts Glaze A add—1 part Glaze B
—2 parts ,, ,,
—3 ,, ,, ,,
—4 ,, ,, ,,
(equal parts) —5 ,, ,, ,,

75

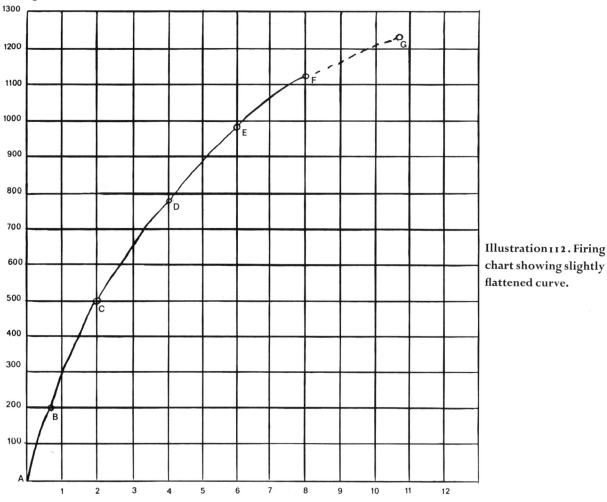

Centigrade temperature

Hours of firing

Illustration 112. Firing chart showing slightly flattened curve.

2nd SERIES

To 5 parts Glaze B add—1 part Glaze A
     —2 parts ,, ,,
     —3 ,, ,, ,,
     —4 ,, ,, ,,
(equal parts) —5 ,, ,, ,,

A test is made, on a disc or curved tile, of the full-strength glazes and of each variation. The proportions will not be mathematically exact, since some of the glaze is taken up on each trial and the two "equal parts" tests will be marginally different, but the system gives you a picture of the important stages between the glaze limits. Carrying a single series beyond "equal parts" uses a lot of glaze and leads to arithmetical complications. It is always easier to start a second series from the other end. It is *important to stir* each mixture thoroughly and to observe the golden rule—one alteration at a time. Do not, for instance, alter the firing temperature or clay body within one glaze test series.

EXAMPLE OF A SERIES

An exhaustive and rewarding series of opaque colored earthenware glaze was carried out using the six primary pigments: oxides of tin, copper, antimony, manganese, cobalt and iron at "saturation" level in a common 1994° F. (1090° C.) foundation glaze. Additional variety was introduced with a low-firing frit (see page 77) which melts at 1832° F. (1000° C.).

The first series mixed each colored glaze with the white (tin) glaze and the frit. The second and much longer sequence combined the colored glazes two at a time and repeated the additions of tin glaze and frit.

All tests were fired on buff and red clay discs. The whole series involved 90 odd, quite distinct glaze colors, each of which could be worked back by simple arithmetic to a reasonably close recipe. All bits of mixed glaze can be combined and need not be wasted.

KILN GRAPHS

Kiln graphs are further records which are both useful and of great interest when testing a new kiln or wiring system. They tell you what has happened and forecast what would happen if the firing were prolonged, whether the kiln is likely to reach a desired temperature, and so on. For really accurate curves one needs a pyrometer, but in testing an earthenware glaze a cone pat made from three cones (covering the top 662° F. (350° C.) or so) will give a good indication, e.g. 015, 05 and 3. A single top temperature reading will not reveal a curve and a straight line is inaccurate and misleading.

The graph chart (see Illustration 112) consists simply of squares on paper. For most occasions 13 lines each way is sufficient. The readings—upwards from the bottom left-hand corner—represent degrees of Centigrade, those across hours of firing.

The slowly flattening curve (plotted on the chart) is typical of all firings and is caused by increasing heat loss through the bricks, etc.

Graphs, correlated with glaze results, can suggest reasons for faults or can assist in the repetition of a desired result. With a pyrometer a *cooling* graph might be of value and would certainly be of interest.

TECHNIQUES OF GLAZING

It is probable that more pieces are spoiled during glazing than at any other stage. That "it will all smooth out in the firing" is a common delusion. Certainly some glazes are more accommodating than others: differences of thickness in a clear glaze may be difficult to detect, while variations in an opaque or colored glaze will show clearly. Bubbling, crazing and other ills can often be traced to faulty glaze application. In any case, the tidier a piece looks when it goes into the kiln, the better it is likely to look when it comes out.

TYPES OF GLAZE

Frits: These are ready-prepared glazes and are, in fact, powdered glass. They will behave somewhat differently from "raw" glazes in handling and firing. For instance, a thinner coating is advisable. A "suspender" (generally a silicate of soda, or water-glass), to prevent the powder sinking to the bottom of its container during use, will help in the glaze batch. Ask the supplier of the frit for advice on this.

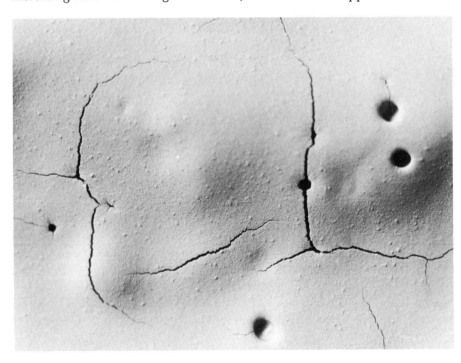

Illustration 113. Close-up of a surface coated with badly stirred glaze. Cracks are likely to break apart during firing.

Illustration 114. Partially glazed pebble form. Stoneware.

Raw glaze: The actual mineral constituents of a glaze, mixed together in water. Most hand-potters are agreed that this results in better quality and a greater sense of integration with the clay. Also it is possible to alter a raw material glaze to suit your clay or firing conditions, and it is easier to handle during and after application.

THICKNESS OF GLAZE

The deposit of powder left on the surface of a pot after it has been dipped is due to the biscuit having absorbed water so that the glaze thickens locally and adheres to the pot. There are several factors which influence the amount of glaze which will be deposited. The principal ones are:

(a) the porosity of the biscuit
(b) the thickness of the glaze mixture
(c) the speed of glazing
(d) the thickness of the clay wall.

Porosity of biscuit can be checked by applying the tip of your tongue to it. If your tongue seems to stick slightly, the biscuit is fairly porous and will take glaze readily; if it

feels smooth and stays wet, the biscuit has been high-fired and will need a thicker glaze mixture to balance its low porosity. The principle may more readily be appreciated if we imagine attempting to coat a fired glazed surface. Here the porosity is nil and a normal glaze mixture will drain off, leaving the surface almost clear.

The consistency of the glaze mixture should be such that its surface immediately returns to its level when a stick is drawn through it, but should leave an opaque deposit on a dry finger which has been dipped into it. Within these limits it will need to be a little thinner (more water added) if the biscuit is very porous or the pot has thick walls. Industrially, glaze (and slip) is discussed in terms of ounces of dry material per pint of water. Generally, this is between 24 and 30. A weighted, upright float called a hydrometer is used to test consistency. A simple version can be made fairly easily (see page 75).

Speed of glazing: A pot or dish whipped quickly through a glaze will have time to absorb only a minimum of water. If the glazing is done slowly, a thicker coating will be

78

deposited. If done *too* slowly, or if the piece is damp, the glaze may fail to dry owing to the saturation of the biscuit. There is more danger of this happening on very thin-walled pieces.

Conclusions:

Thinner mixtures for:
    frits
    porous biscuit
    thick-walled pieces
    slow glazing
    also, in general, clear glazes.

Thicker mixtures for:
    higher-fired low porosity biscuit
    very thin-walled pieces
    skimming tiles
    also, in general, opaque glazes.

From experience you will learn that there is an ideal thickness for each glaze.

APPLYING THE GLAZE

Speed and smoothness of movement are the keys to good glazing. Think carefully before starting each piece and work out the best procedure. There are several techniques.

1. *Immersing.* The easiest and quickest way for dishes and pots where there is plenty of glaze and the piece is not too large. Hold a pot by the rim (one finger or thumb) and the base (two fingers). Hold a dish with one finger on one side of the rim and two on the other. Sweep the dish (with the further edge entering the glaze first) down, through, up and out, like a diver. Hold vertically to drain and stand down on a stilt. If the fingers are previously dipped in glaze, little touchups will be unnecessary, but what there is to do, do quickly before the glaze dries if possible.

2. *Rolling.* For pots, beakers, etc., in a shallow glaze. Hold with two fingers on the base and two on the rim and "walk" them round the pot so that it revolves in the glaze. Tip right way up for a moment to ensure covering inside the base, then invert to drain. Set down on a stilt.

3. *Skimming.* For tiles. Hold across the back with fingers and thumb in order to skim the tile across the glaze, the leading edge touching first. With practice, a neat glaze line along the edges can be achieved.

4. *Pouring.* With large pots it is often neces-

Illustration 115. Glazing a dish by immersion.

Illustration 116. Rolling a pot in a shallow bowl of glaze.

sary to pour the glaze over the outside. Use a good-sized jug or pitcher for glaze. If it can be gripped, hold the pot upside down, as far around as possible in one direction so that a smooth and complete turn can be made as the glaze is poured. Use a large bowl to catch surplus. If the pot is too heavy to hold, it can be supported on a long stick and turned, or else on supports in a bowl on a turntable.

5. *Spraying.* Blowing glaze through a spray is dangerous—a bulb or mechanical pump should be used, ideally with an extractor fan. It takes a good deal of spraying to achieve a thick enough glaze coating, but for slip-glazes and thin layers and for certain special effects it can be useful, although always resulting in a somewhat mechanical finish.

6. *"Water-spout" method.* This takes some practice (try it when washing up!), but is ideal for the quick glazing of beakers, wide-mouthed pots, bowls, etc., particularly for stonewares. The piece is gripped by the foot or base, dipped to the desired level outside, then sharply lifted straight up until it just leaves the glaze, the suction causing a "water-spout" to rise. Very quickly the pot is pushed down onto the rising column of glaze which will coat the interior of even tall jugs evenly and completely. (After trying it, you will probably add "sometimes!") But with practice it is a very reliable method.

7. *Fill and dip.* A satisfactory alternative if the "water-spout" is found to be too difficult. Hold the pot by the foot, right way up, fill it with glaze from a jug, tip the glaze out and immediately plunge into a bin or bowl of glaze.

SOME GENERAL NOTES

Pour some of the clean water from the top of a glaze before stirring. Keep handy in a jug and re-add if necessary.

Stir your glaze *very thoroughly*. Keep stirred during use.

Label permanent containers clearly with type of glaze and a code number or actual recipe.

Beware changing containers when re-sieving a glaze, which is necessary from time to time.

Use a container of suitable size and shape for the piece to be glazed.

80

Illustration 117.
Skimming a tile. Keep the glaze well stirred and the surface free of bubbles.

Touch up holding marks with finger or brush immediately after glazing. Smooth repair over as it dries. Tongs or grips will minimize marks.

Carefully scrape down bad runs or blotches of glaze with a sharp, thin-bladed knife or tool (a photographic retouching knife is excellent) soon after glazing.

It is easier to protect a surface from glaze than to scrape it off afterward. The flange of a lidded pot, for instance, can be waxed, or the holes at the base of a teapot spout can be covered with a pad of clay (be sure to remove it afterward).

Glazing is a critical and important stage in the making of a pot and should be given as much care, thought and attention as the designing, throwing and decoration.

EXPERIMENTS WITH GLAZES

There are hundreds of ready-made glazes, many of them excellent. Why then try to make your own? The answer probably is that it is difficult to resist seeing what happens if we add a bit here, or alter a recipe there, fire a little higher, or a little lower. Those who experiment with glazes are sustained by curiosity and optimism. The background of chemicals and fire is very similar to that of the old alchemists. Indeed, it was an ironical twist of fate which led the German, Bottger, who was more or less imprisoned while trying to transmute metals to develop European porcelain, to a discovery which probably created as much wealth as would turning lead into gold.

As mentioned earlier, ready-made glazes are *frits*, that is, the ingredients have already been melted together into glass and the glass ground down into a fine powder which is the material you buy. Frits may be divided into three types:

1. Complete glazes to be used without additions;

2. Low temperature glazes to which raw materials may be added;

3. Simple ingredients fritted because they may be (a) poisonous on their own, such as the oxide of lead, or (b) soluble in water, or subject to liquefying, as is boric oxide.

81

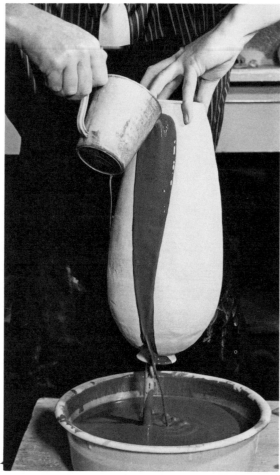

Illustration 118
Pouring glaze over a large pot supported on a
stick.

For many ingredients you can use natural materials (minerals) which are often readily available in a fairly pure, insoluble form (calcium oxide and silica, for instance). For others you can use what might be called "natural frits"—rocks which were melted together millions of years ago and have since broken down or decomposed into powder, or which can be ground into powder. Some potters actually grind suitable rocks which yield fine glazes. Harry Davies had a large water-driven crusher which provided him with superb celadon porcelain glaze. He is now doing the same thing with the rich lava deposits of New Zealand. In the East they found that the white ashes of wood and grasses contained the makings of high tem-

perature glazes. The fire had burned away all the organic matter and left, in effect, a frit of the minerals contained in the plant.

Although it may seem that all has been discovered in the way of glazes, even small variations in the composition or firing temperature will show markedly different results and it is still possible to achieve novel surfaces and types of glaze. The realization that the element life of an electric kiln would be longer if stoneware firings could stop short of 2282° F. (1250° C.) led me to develop a range of glazes maturing at 2246-2264° F. (1230–1240° C.) which are not quite like any used before.

The simplest successful result in glazemaking is exciting and satisfying, while even "unsuccessful" glazes can start you on a new track. For the beginner probably with no knowledge of chemistry, the problems posed by books on glazes may seem insurmountable. But theory is only part of the game—the proof is in the kiln. All pre-industrial potters made up their glazes by rule-of-thumb.

BASIC GLAZE TESTS

A simple earthenware glaze need comprise three common raw materials only. These could be:

1. Lead oxide (fritted). Coated lead sesquisilicate or bisilicate recommended.

2. Clay. Try any clay from red clay to China clay.

3. Flint. Powdered flint pebbles obtained as a white powder from most suppliers. A form of pure silica.

Without going into details, the principal action of these materials in the formation of glass is as follows:

1. Lead oxide is the "melting agent." An increase will lower the melting point (firing temperature) of the glaze.

2. Clay acts chiefly as a "binding agent." It will steady the glaze and help it to adhere to the pot. As a secondary effect, an increase will tend to produce a matte surface.

3. Flint is the "bone" of the glaze. It is the foundation of all glazes from the softest to the hardest. An increase will tend to "harden" or raise the melting point of the glaze.

Start your glaze tests by:

1. Testing each material on its own.

2. Testing simple mixtures. Let us say, one test with equal proportions, and three others each with one material in excess.

In table form:

Ingredient	Experiment number						
	1	2	3	4	5	6	7
Frit	100			33	80	10	10
Clay		100		33	10	80	10
Flint			100	33	10	10	80

Be sure to keep a careful note of work done, preferably in pottery pigment on the test piece itself. For these trials 300 grams (10 ounces) will suffice, but for later more subtle combinations, up to 1000 grams is advisable.

Note that the above columns all add up to about 100. They can therefore be treated as percentages which makes for easier calculation and comparison.

To make 300 grams, multiply each figure by three: for 500, multiply throughout by 5, and so on.

To make 10 ounces (if grams not available) divide throughout by 10. Column 4 thus becomes 3.3 or 3⅓ ounces; column 6, 1 ounce, 8 ounces and 1 ounce, respectively.

Weigh materials carefully, mix together in water, and pass through a 120-mesh sieve. You can use plenty of water for the sieving so that no material is lost. The glaze will soon settle and surplus liquid can be poured off. Glaze a test piece, perferably a standing section of a cylinder, coated about halfway down. An adequate and even thickness of glaze is essential if the test is really going to tell the truth about the mixture.

Normally, tests **are** made on biscuit but you can also try the **mixtures** on leather-hard clay, using them like slip. Try brushing some on thinly. Watch the glaze coating during drying and discard it if it comes away from the pot through excessive or too little shrinkage. Fire the tests accurately—2012° F. (1000° C.) is a good standard temperature for earthenwares.

It is advisable to stand the test pieces on a layer of calcined alumina in case the **glaze** runs badly.

Illustration 119. This dish, held by wire grips, has had its base waxed to resist the glaze.

83

Illustration 120
A garden layout using glazed tiles with circular holes and slab and coiled dishes to hold various small plants. Glazed ceramic works contrast sharply with small pebbles.

ASSESSMENT OF THE RESULTS

1. Do any of the trials look like glazes, and which mixture is nearest the goal of a clear transparent glaze? (Note: red clay or colored slip on test pieces will help you to decide just how transparent a glaze is.)

2. If a true glaze has not been formed, is the result interesting in its own right? There are a number of mixtures which are neither quite slip or glaze but embody some characteristics of both. These are sometimes called "engobes." These in-between mixtures are more likely to be successful at higher temperatures.

3. Has the glaze managed to stay on the pot, or will it peel or crack if tapped with a piece of wood? If it lifts or has lifted during firing, this may be due to the shrinkage rate and an alteration in clay content could help. Red clay generally, has the greatest shrinkage, China clay the least. The use of red clay in the recipe will give a warmer color to the glaze which is excellent for slipware.

4. Consider the firing temperature. Could this be adjusted to improve the result? A little higher to completely melt the glaze, lower if it has run or bubbled.

ADJUSTING THE RECIPE

In the light of the information given earlier concerning the action of the materials used in this series, you can now begin to modify the experiments in purposeful directions. For instance, adding frit if the glaze looks immature, rough, or not quite transparent, adding more clay or flint if it looks too soft, has bubbled, or run. There is one Golden Rule in making any change to a recipe. *Alter only one material at a time.* Otherwise, you can never be sure which modification has been effective.

The foregoing series embodies only one melting (fusing) agent—lead oxide. It is the type often used on slipware and hand-built wares, especially on red clay. It is less successful for painted surfaces, sometimes causing the color to run. It can be colored with the usual pigment oxides and opacified with tin, titanium, or zircon. It is essentially the glaze used by the country potters of England and Europe from medieval times, the lead generally being provided by "galena," a lead sulphide, which is somewhat less poisonous than some raw leads. Although it is possible to apply the glaze straight onto the dry clay pots, it is a technique not recommended on our rather more pervious clays, although spraying onto the nearly dry clay can be a useful finish for large pots, firing to about 2102° F. (1150° C.).

The first rule of glazemaking illustrated by these experiments is that all glazes contain:

1. Silica (contained in many minerals, and pure in the form of flint, quartz and sand);

2. Alumina (contained in clay and some other minerals. Note: the calcined alumina mentioned above is too coarse for use in glazes);

3. Flux. At least one flux.

Most glazes are more complex than this example, but the rule always holds and the experimental pattern can be used as a model for trying other materials. Perhaps replacing lead frit with a soft leadless one.

Illustration 121. Interestingly glazed slab tray.

GLAZE INGREDIENTS

You may now be wondering why, if a simple frit plus clay and flint will make a glaze, it is necessary to bring in other and more complicated materials, and why some glaze formulas or recipes list five or more ingredients. The full answer would take many pages, but briefly:

• There are many subtle variations of glaze surface and general character.

• A simple glaze may have a tendency to run or bubble.

• The shrinkage may need adjustment to suit the clay body and so minimize crazing.

• The glaze constituents, especially the fluxes, will have a marked effect on any coloring pigment.

• Some of the more complicated glazes can be applied more thinly without appearing starved. Compare a piece of slipware with a commercial cup.

A glaze used over underglaze painting or as a basis for opaque white or self-color will generally contain more than one flux. The frit itself will contain more than one melting agent. Any earthenware glaze firing up to 2102° F. (1150° C.) which has no lead oxide will certainly contain borax as a principal ingredient. Unfortunately, borax is a difficult material to use on its own and must be stabilized as a frit.

In lead frit glazes, there are two more commonly used minerals, both of which have some fluxing action. These are feldspar and whiting.

EARTHENWARE GLAZE TEST

Add these ingredients to your other materials and try some tests. The number of trials necessary to cover the range by "rule of thumb" alone is considerably increased by these additions, and it might be much better to use the more accurate and scientific methods of compounding and testing each variation of your glaze.

You might try: (1) firing the feldspar and whiting alone; (2) progressively increasing the frit proportion; (3) increasing the feldspar content considerably (to 25%) and lowering the maximum frit proportion. This will test how far the feldspar will replace lead frit as a flux.

Also, try leaving flint out entirely and juggle with the remaining ingredients, still keeping feldspar fairly high.

These tests give a reasonable coverage of *likely* combinations as distinct from purely arbitrary ones, using the results of the first series as a guide.

A word of explanation for the omission of flint in one of your tests. Flint in its pure form is silica and silica is contained in the frit itself, which is a melted mixture of lead oxide and flint. Silica also is present in feldspar and clay. Thus, these three sources supply the flint needed.

The mixture you finally decide will be the most successful should be suitable for tin (opaque white) glaze techniques and for colored glazes.

Feldspar can be replaced by China Stone, a similar mineral. The latter will tend to brighten colors applied to the glaze, but may also increase crazing tendencies. It is also a little more refractory than feldspar.

There is another important rule to remember when compounding glazes. A number of fluxes used together will melt a glaze more efficiently than any one used alone.

Illustration 122
Japanese symbol for "a raku firing." Calligraphy by
Hidei Iwata.

10. Raku

keynote of the well-planned raku session—this "conscious return to the direct and primitive treatment of clay" (Leach).

The technique and esthetics of raku is at the opposite pole to the clean, controlled work from an electric kiln, for raku ware biscuited and glazed is placed in an already-hot kiln and is fired in a quick reduction atmosphere. It may be a little difficult at first to adjust to the different qualities of raku and its method of firing.

It is many years since Bernard Leach in his "Potters Book" introduced a chapter with: "Raku . . . brings the making of pots within the range of any enthusiast." But in England it has taken the brazier kiln of David Ballantyne and raku enthusiasts John Chalke and Murray Fieldhouse to spark off the current increase of activity in England in this field of ceramics.

It was raku which first brought Leach into ceramics, with the resultant explosion of interest in the Western world in non-industrial pottery.

The Japanese symbol for raku ware means "enjoyment and happiness," and this is the

Illustration 123
Raku bowl by Ann Gretton made at a raku party.

87

Illustration 124
A raku party can have added excitement at night.

GIVING A RAKU PARTY

The best, perhaps the only, way to fully enjoy this coarse-bodied, porous, yet fascinating ware is to see it through from the building of the kiln to the steaming, glazed pot. All the steps can be achieved in a day.

Probably only heavy rain could spoil a raku party. Darkness can help since the glowing kiln is then more evident and exciting at night.

THE POTS

There is some conflict of opinion on the appropriate style for raku pottery, but there is no reason why a considered and even sophisticated design cannot be introduced. The typical raku piece tends, however, to be fairly thick, asymmetric, and generally hand-built.

Thrown bowls and other fairly open shapes are possible, as well as dishes of all types. Cut corner dishes described in the chapter on Pottery Dishes Without Molds would be suitable as well as pinched pots and slabware. The often considerable richness of color and surface obtained by the painting, the glaze and the subsequent reduction means that excessive texturing or embossing of the clay surface is not essential. The Japanese prototypes are usually simple, well proportioned forms with smooth surfaces. However, try everything and analyze the results afterwards.

The clay body must be open and well-grogged, but need not be as coarse as is sometimes used. It is subject to sudden and considerable strain in the very short firing cycle.

88

Illustration 125
Section through a top-loading raku brazier kiln (top) with indication of position of bricks supporting sagger (below).

A recipe for raku ware from David Rhodes' "Clay and Glazes for the Potter" is:

Stoneware clay	30%
Fire clay	25%
Ball clay	15%
Feldspar	5%
Flint	5%
Grog	20%

Grogged fire clay or a 60–40 mixture of ball clay and medium grog (60 to 40 mesh sieve) also can be used with the addition of about 10% china clay to whiten if required.

The pots are normally made previous to the raku session and biscuited to 1652–1832° F. (900–1000° C.). For a few pots it is possible to biscuit in the raku kiln itself, packing before firing starts, but this severely limits the pieces available for glazing and loses the point of the firings which are repeated every 20 minutes or so for two or three hours.

THE GLAZE

Almost any glaze which will melt at the temperature normally obtained—1382–1562°F. (750–850° C.)—is suitable. A white lead/quartz recipe is given in "A Potters Book." The lowest temperature frits easily obtainable are lead sesquisilicate (monosilicate would probably lower the silica ratio too far) and other high lead frits. These have the advantage of less shrinkage in the raw glaze coat and less backing in the fire. David Rhodes gives this formula:

White lead	55%
Flint	25%
Feldspar	10%
Clay	5%
Whiting	5%

Together with a suitable siccative such as $\frac{1}{2}$% gum arabic, this will give a starting point for experiment. Bentonite is also recommended (about 2%) to give body to the frits.

Any coloring oxides can be used as pigment for painting onto or under the glaze or added to the glaze batch itself as in normal firing. Tin will opacify, as in a majolica glaze. Chrome is useful.

Enamels and gold enamel can be used with discretion. The contrast with the rough clay is often stimulating.

Illustration 126
Front-loading raku kiln with sagger door in place and glazed pots drying.

89

Illustration 127
A small pot is loaded into the red-hot, square-built, top-loading raku kiln.

Glaze reasonably thickly and do not leave too great an area of body unglazed. One glaze can be poured over another, in which case both glazes will need to be thinner in consistency.

THE KILN

The original Japanese kilns resembled the Roman type—a long firemouth feeding into a round chamber containing a perforated raised hearth. Long flame wood was necessary for firing. The "brazier" kiln developed by David Ballantyne is more simple and flexible, being no more than a dry-built brick cylinder containing a sagger (a box made of fireclay in which delicate articles to be fired are placed). Coke, between the sagger and the bricks, heats the muffle and the pots put into it. Draft is supplied through spaces left between the bricks.

In plan, the kiln and sagger may be circular, oval, or square. There is some preference for the circular kiln. A circle of eight bricks with one-inch spaces gives a reasonable size kiln, but this must be varied to suit the diameter of the sagger. The coke space all around should be equal roughly to half the diameter of the sagger. Pots are loaded into the red-hot sagger from above.

A variant has a side opening muffle (Illustration 126). In constructing the kiln a dry hearth is advisable in the form of bricks or a metal sheet. On this the sagger is positioned on three bricks $4\frac{1}{2}$ inches from the ground. Around it the wall is built simply by standing one brick on another to a height of 12 inches above the sagger lid. Two or three of the bottom bricks should be placed sideways and the construction above them must stand firm when they are removed. This is to enable spent coke debris to be raked out during firing. Over the whole kiln a roof (sheet metal but not cast iron) will probably be found necessary to build up the initial heat. Galvanized iron may release arsenic fumes.

THE SAGGER

The sagger may be of any ceramic material and may be purchased from any ceramic or refractory supply house. A home-made sagger may be coiled from a material similar to that used for the pots. It needs to be strong, of even thickness and with a very close-fitting lid held on with two stout loop handles. Long-handled hooks made to fit these loops are useful for removing the red-hot lid.

EQUIPMENT AND MATERIALS

Use cheap open *bricks*. Close dark bricks may blow and cause damage. Do *not* use concrete in any part of the kiln. *Coke* must be medium grade, for small coke will clog the fire. *Wood* should be dry and easily ignitable (fir is good but brushwood will do). *Tongs* with handles at least 3 feet long will be essential for packing and removing pots. *Hooks* for the sagger lid (mentioned above) and a *flat-ended tool* for raking coke are useful. *Asbestos gloves* will protect your hands.

Incidentals include: *extra bricks* for standing done pots, sagger lids, etc., *metal buckets* or *tin*

Illustration 128
More usual form of top-loading kiln into which glazed piece is being placed with long tongs.

Illustration 129
Raku dish, red-hot from kiln, is immersed in peat to create reduction effects.

baths for dowsing water, and *sawdust*, *peat* or *grass* in suitable non-inflammable containers for reduction.

FIRING

Firing of the raku ware decorated by the guests is the heart of the matter and the climax of a raku party. The fire is started with wood or firelighters (a little coal is useful to get it under way) and slowly built up until the glowing coke covers the lid of the sagger. This will take about two hours and note must be taken of wind direction and force. The draft openings will have to be altered or a fireproof baffle put up to control burning. The pots are glazed and stacked on the lid or perimeter of the kiln to

be *very thoroughly dried*. Give the pots half a turn after several minutes.

The coke is now scraped from the lid which is removed, and pots lowered into the glowing sagger with tongs. The removal of a few top bricks to the leeward of the kiln (Illustration 127) will facilitate loading and removing. It is not necessary to have the pots separated as in a normal kiln load, although this can be done if desired. The pots will expand as they warm up, so be careful not to stack them in, or they or the sagger will have to give!

After about 15 minutes, remove the lid and inspect the glazes. If they are melted, the sheen will be apparent. The alkaline glaze will bubble and the ware will be ready for removal when it has settled down again. If the glaze is not "done" (a trial can be removed to make sure) continue the firing for a further 10 minutes.

When the pots are removed from the kiln with tongs, they can be dowsed immediately in water and the resultant hissing and steaming is a great part of the spectacle. With water treatment only, the body and glaze will be normal "oxidized." On the other hand, if the glowing pot is immersed in or partly covered with peat or sawdust, it will be "reduced" and carbonized; the body will go black and the colors, especially if copper has been used, become iridescent or metallic with many variations.

Several firings can take place in quick succession, but clinker and ash will eventually build up and will need to be raked out from below. In order to maintain sagger temperature, wood is used until the coke, stoked in from the top, is again burning well.

Finally, the pots are *well scrubbed* to remove carbon deposits from reduction, revealing glazes and colors.

Like all pottery techniques, the results of raku sessions will improve with practice and experience, but even if your first raku does not produce a bowl fit for exhibit, it is bound to give enjoyment and some excitement to all who take part in it and will lead to a more genuine appreciation of the nature of fire and glaze than will any amount of peering through the spy-hole of an electric kiln where the forces at work are tamed and hidden.

11. Starting a Pottery Workshop

Pottery students frequently ask: "How can I start up on my own studio—and how much would it cost?" There is no simple answer.

The first consideration is the fundamental one of purpose, for on this all questions of equipment depend. The student may have studied ceramics at an art school or university and no longer have access to a studio, or he may still be a member of a class, experiencing the familiar frustrations of lack of continuity, scrambling for firing space, and so on. In any case, it is natural to think of the advantage of having one's own workshop.

It is true that a small workshop of one's own can be a great pleasure, but it is worth looking into a little further. For instance, there is the question of what to do with the produced pots. In even a small studio, quite a lot is turned out and it would be misleading to suggest that there is a ready market in the shops for the non-professional potter. Again, pause to consider how much you have really learned about the practical things—loading, firing, glaze mixing and experiment, slips, clays and so on. Gaps in one's knowledge become very evident when you are really on your own. Books can be useful, but the best advice would be to continue at your classes while you are setting up your workshop so that you can ask about problems as they arise. Concentrated short courses can be useful as they often take place in well equipped workshops.

When, despite the obvious obstacles, you decide to go ahead, try to concentrate your field of activity. In even a large set-up, with individual rooms for making, glazing, and firing, it is difficult to combine many techniques. One can soon accumulate so many buckets, jars and bowls of materials that there is no room for pots. Your skill and consequent pleasure in the work will develop more rapidly if your workshop remains quite severely limited in scope.

It is this exploration in depth which is the first step to really rewarding and significant work. Of course, more than one technique or style should be attempted, but, for practical reasons as well as esthetic, try one at a time and give each aspect of ceramics the time to develop and mature. Original ideas do not often come through sitting and thinking but more likely are the by-products of work.

KILN

Whether your choice for a start is slipware, modeling, tableware, slab work, or any other of the many branches of pottery, there is one primary piece of equipment common to all—a kiln. It is the firing which distinguishes ceramics from all other arts.

A wheel, which so many put first on the list, is obviously desirable but it is secondary. With a working surface, clay, and a kiln, the scope is enormous.

So let's deal with the kiln first. The safest form of heating is electricity. Gas and oil kilns tend to come in larger sizes and the chimney hazard is considerable, although new possibilities are arising with the use of propane or cylinder gases. Electric kilns are available from a few inches high to three feet and at a wide range of prices.

All parts of a stoneware kiln, not only the elements, need to be sturdier than a low-firing equivalent. One way to get a high performance kiln at low performance cost is to make it yourself (see the next chapter) but there are many good electric kilns available.

POWER SUPPLY

The question of power supply is important. Small kilns can utilize standard 110-volt power lines. Larger sizes require special wiring and the electric company may require (as well as the kiln) a 220-volt power line. Installation of this will add considerably to the cost. Sacrifice may have to be made in cost, space, or temperature, depending upon the type of work you intend to do.

RUNNING COSTS

Working out the running costs of firing depends partly on the speed at which the required temperature is reached with the kiln on at high, and it would be advisable to ask the kiln manufacturer about this. Then do the following sum: multiply the kilowatt rating of the kiln by the number of hours required to fire (at full) by the price of electricity per kilowatt-hour. To be realistic add an amount on to cover the wear and tear on elements and kiln furniture. Divide the cost of a complete set of new elements by 80 (a guess at the average life); the cost of the kiln itself by 300; and the cost of the shelves and so on by 100. Add a few pennies to cover cones, etc., and determine your firing costs per cubic foot for both biscuit and glaze firing.

KILN AREA

It is not entirely advantageous to have your kiln in your workshop. Certainly it is convenient and keeps you warm occasionally in the winter, but there are also the problems of fumes which some clays give off, the humidity at stages of biscuit firing, and the smoke from wax resist, etc.

Wherever the kiln is put should be reasonably well ventilated.

The workshop itself may take so many forms that only a general discussion is possible. It is a question of suiting your ambitions to the practical possibilities. A small room, say, 8 feet × 11 feet, if worked out with care and kept in very good order can suffice for a limited scope of activity, but a space of at least 130 square feet (13 feet × 10 feet) is needed to

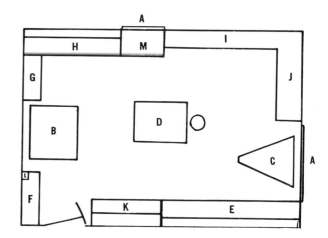

Illustration 130

A typical layout recommended for a small pottery workshop, 16 feet by 11 feet.

Code:

A. Windows. Roof-lights are also recommended over E and B.

B. Kiln. Capacity up to 18-inch cube.

C. Wheel.

D. Table.

E. Wedging and working bench, wooden surface. 6-inch shelves over for materials.

F. 12-inch deep shelving for kiln equipment.

G. 12-inch deep shelving for biscuit and glazed pots.

H. Bench and draining board. 6-inch shelves over for glaze materials, colors, etc. Space under for glaze bins.

I.J. Shelving. For drying pots and work in progress. Space under for clay bins (J), materials or glazes.

K. Display area. For finished work. 18-inch bench with 9-inch shelves over. Cupboard under, for storage of finished work.

M. Sink.

L. Power point, switchgear, etc., for kiln.

This layout keeps the wet work as far as possible from the kiln and provides a work sequence starting from the wedging bench E through throwing, drying, biscuit, and glaze.

A separate display area may seem a luxury but it can have great value.

avoid too many frustrations, and 15 feet × 12 feet would be more comfortable. See Illustration 130 for a typical layout.

WORKING SURFACE AND SHELVES

As mentioned before, a sound working surface, preferably of wood is the only absolute essential for a studio. Next on the list should come the shelves, fairly deep, possibly adaptable and movable.

There are two systems involving doweling which are fairly simple to construct. The first consists of two 2-inch × 1½-inch uprights fastened to the wall about 2 feet apart and drilled for ¾-inch dowels. The doweling stands out about 9 inches from the battens, and wooden shelves simply rest on them so that the shelves themselves are completely transportable.

A more permanent, but still adaptable, variant is to make ladders of 2-inch × 1-inch timber with ½-inch dowels across at 4-inch intervals. These can be joined top and bottom with cross pieces to form a rectangular frame. Shelves, either of board, or more cheaply of lengths of 2 inch × 1 inch nailed to 12-inch battens can be supported on the dowel "rungs" at the required distance apart to

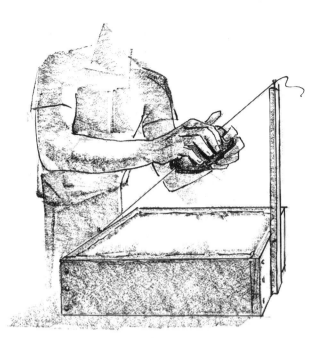

Drawing by Louis Di Valentin, from "Practical Encyclopedia of Crafts."

Illustration 132
A wedging board is a vital piece of equipment in any studio. This one can be constructed easily.

suit the work being produced at any time. This type of shelving can be on any depth, but 18 inches is as wide as normally required and 12 inches is average. Illustration 131 shows shelving of this sort in a small workroom. It is useful to have a space of about 2 to 2½ feet below any shelving to accommodate bins and sacks of material and glazes.

A wedge board is also a good investment and an essential tool in the workshop.

WATER

A sink and water supply make life so much easier in a pottery studio that they should come next on your list. Remember to have your tap high enough to put large buckets under.

WHEELS

The fifth major item is the wheel. Here again, if you are reasonably handy (but in no sense skilled) with tools, you can build a "tailored," seated, side kick wheel with a 50-pound flywheel. There is not a great deal to choose between the commercial kick wheels although they vary widely in design. Stand-up types of kick wheels are tiring and add extra

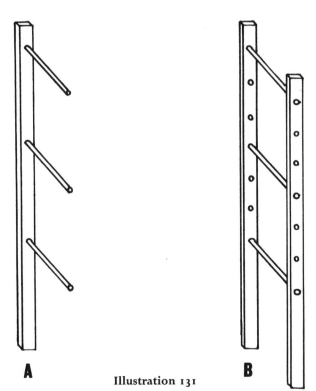

A   **B**

Illustration 131
Two types of home-made shelving: a. Doweling set in uprights. b. Ladder construction using thinner dowels.

Drawings by Louis Di Valentin, from "Practical Encyclopedia of Crafts."

Illustration 133
Useful equipment for the workshop includes (top)
a "wet box" or a rubber-covered drum (middle)
for storing clay, and (below) a kick wheel.

problems of balance and body movement to the already difficult technique of throwing.

With power wheels it is easier to stand and work, and many potters prefer these. There are a number of different kinds on the market. In any case it is a good idea to ask the manufacturers of various wheels for the address of a local school or pottery which has the equipment being considered. You can then see it and discuss its advantages and snags.

THE PUGMILL

The pugmill is another item you may wish to consider for your studio but most potters do not use it in a small studio. This is a mechanical mixer with propeller-like blades which cut up the clay and force it into a narrowing tube from which it issues in a long coil. A really efficient pugmill is expensive and bulky. It must be said, however, that a pugmill is not magic and that very hard and soft clay put into it will come out still hard and soft though more broken up and blended. It is advisable always to get the clay as near to a good plastic state as possible by stiffening very wet material and soaking dry lumps.

MATERIALS

The suggestion of initially limiting the scope of the studio is of prime importance and applies also to the ordering of supplies—clays, oxides, etc. The second rule regarding materials is to buy your materials in quantities as large as is convenient to store. This has two advantages: (1) you get to know the behavior of that particular batch of material in handling and firing (natural minerals such as clay, feldspar, etc., only approximate their ideal formula, and even frit can vary); (2) the saving in costs can be considerable. For example, almost all supplies are much cheaper per pound when ordered in large or medium-sized quantities.

Order clay in polyethylene bags rather than string and paper wrapping. It is considerably cheaper this way and the cleaned bags make excellent storage for your dry materials. The aim is to get clay which is as "natural" as possible. The white clays often supplied by ceramic suppliers are industrial bodies with no

Illustration 134

Corner of a workshop fitted with ladder-type construction shelving. Potter is working on wooden table, making hand-built pots started in biscuit bowls used as molds.

"bite" or character and are comparatively low in true plasticity. Many professional potters order direct from the clay suppliers and blend their own mixtures with sand, etc. You may find local clays which are adequate, especially for earthenware.

Apart from clays, you will need glaze materials, oxides, frits, etc., and a few miscellaneous materials for the kiln. It is more fun and, in the long run gives more individual results, to make up your own glazes from raw materials. This type of glaze also has better suspension and coating strength. The ingredients for your glazes need not be numerous—perhaps half a dozen for earthenware and a similar number for stoneware (some being common to both).

Brushwork and the color of slips and glazes, involve pigments—all oxides of metals—and, as with glazes, you have the choice of buying them ready-made for specific purposes (underglaze, glaze, stains, etc.) or getting a few raw materials (from which they are all made anyhow) and learning to use them yourself.

Here are four suggested ordering lists for specific techniques. The weights are suggested *minimums*. As previously recommended, buy more if you can. They also indicate the rough *proportional* quantities you may use. Prices will vary due to quantity and there is usually an additional freight charge.

Chart A: Earthenware. Majolica painting and/or underglaze decoration.

	Amount
Plastic buff clay	300 lbs
Lead sesquisilicate or bisilicate	28 lbs
Potash feldspar	14 lbs
China clay	7 lbs
Whiting	7 lbs
Flint	7 lbs
Red iron oxide	1 lb
Copper carbonate	1 lb
Cobalt carbonate	½ lb
Manganese oxide	1 lb
Lead antimoniate	½ lb
Tin oxide	4 lbs

Note: This supposes the use of a lead-lime-potash type glaze recipe with 10% tin oxide for majolica painting or pigment under tin.

Chart B: Earthenware. Slipware and slip-trailing.

	Amount
Plastic red clay	300 lbs
Powdered red clay (see note)	28 lbs
Powdered buff clay	28 lbs
Lead sesquisilicate *or* bisilicate	28 lbs
Potash feldspar	7 lbs
Manganese oxide	3 lbs
Chrome oxide	½ lb
Copper oxide	½ lb

Notes: For traditional slips on red clay. Slips: Red, buff, black (10% manganese), green (1¼% each chrome and copper (blue slip not included as it looks garish on red clay). Glaze: Honeyglaze. Lead-feldspar-red clay. Powdered clay convenient, but you can easily dry and soak plastic clay for making slip.

Chart C: Stoneware. Thrown, modeled and hand-built pots. Oxidized. 2282° F. (1250° C.).

	Amount
Plastic buff clay	300 lbs
Plastic red clay	50 lbs
Potash feldspar	28 lbs
China clay	7 lbs
Grog 30–60	28 lbs
Whiting	7 lbs
Dolomite	7 lbs
Flint	7 lbs
Barium carbonate	7 lbs
Tin oxide	1 lb
Leadless frit *or* borax frit	7 lbs
Iron oxide	4 lbs
Manganese oxide	4 lbs
Cobalt oxide	½ lb

Notes: For plain and colored glazes. Barium causes interesting variations. Frits useful to soften matt glazes and alter effect of pigments.

ADDITIONAL SUPPLIES

You should also obtain some of the following supplies:

1. Calcined alumina which is superior to flint for dusting on kiln shelves in the glaze firing.

2. Zinc oxide. A flux in stoneware.

3. Firing cones. Expendable and can be counted as materials. Much cheaper by the box. Suggested numbers: 05 for biscuit, 01 for earthenware glaze, 6 and 7 for electric-fired stoneware.

Sockets are expensive and can easily be made of clay. It is a good idea to set a number of cones in clay so that they will be dry when you come to use them.

Finally, a note on suppliers. Most ceramic suppliers are reliable. The large ones tend to carry all kinds of materials, others tend to specialize in narrower ranges, so get several price lists and "shop around" for the best value.

Illustration 135
Kiln complete and firing.

12. Building Your Own Kiln

GENERAL PRINCIPLES

Building a working kiln may seem a formidable task, but in fact it involves only an elementary skill with a saw and screwdriver. If you don't have electrical knowledge, and a license, don't try to wire the kiln. Call in an electrician to do this.

Apart from the satisfaction you get in creating your own equipment, you are in a better position to alter the details and balance of the heating elements if, in practice, the kiln fires unevenly, too slowly, or too fast. A kiln can be put together in a couple of days for less than you would pay for a commercially produced kiln.

A pottery kiln is, fundamentally, a simple piece of equipment. If combustible fuels are used for heating—coal, wood, oil or gas—there is the complication of arranging for a free flow of oxygen through the kiln necessitating a chimney and inlet vents, but with electricity

there is direct energy and no combustion takes place. An electrically-heated kiln, therefore, is a totally enclosed box. While it lacks the excitement of other types of kilns, it can be used in almost any room with safety.

The kiln must, of course, be built of materials which will resist a far higher temperature than the hottest firing you may want to do, and this means a ceramic material. It must also retain the heat fed into it. The walls must insulate, that is, resist the passage of heat through them, a property which depends on both the thickness and the type of brick. An insulating brick is usually light in weight and is full of enclosed air pockets. Thickness will depend on the type of ware to be fired. A wall which will, for instance, happily retain the heat necessary for firing enamels, will be totally inefficient for stoneware. The greater the difference in temperature between the inside and the outside of the kiln, the faster the flow of heat. The inner wall must be free from iron or other impurities which will adversely affect the heating elements.

Also, it must be possible to cut slots in the bricks to hold the wire which will heat the kiln. It is possible to obtain cements which are suitable for medium temperatures, and to cast the walls in sections, element slots and all, but the preparation of molds and the critical cement mixes is difficult and hazardous and a far surer system is to cut prepared slabs.

TYPES OF KILNS

There are two basic types of electric kilns—the front-loader and the top-loader. Both are within the scope of the amateur kiln builder and both have advantages and disadvantages.

The kiln with the loading opening in front involves two rather tricky building operations—a roof and a door. With a small kiln these can be circumvented by using a stout kiln shelf to span the top, while the front opening can be bricked up and taken down at each firing. With a larger kiln an arched roof is advisable.

In a kiln filled from above, the roof *is* the door and, since it does not have to bear continual deadweight, kilns up to say 20 inches × 30 inches in plan can be safely spanned with bats for temperatures up to at least 2300° F. (1260° C.). The top-loader has two other advantages. It is low (some half the height of a front-door kiln which must be about 5 feet 6 inches high) and, even with its roof on, is not much more than table height, so that it can be used, very conveniently, as a drying bench when firing or cooling. The elements can completely surround the pots, giving more even and regular firings.

Potters profess strong preferences for one or the other type of kiln, but this can often be a matter of habit. Actually, it is easier to build the top-loader and that is, therefore, the design to begin with.

FACTORS CONTROLLING DESIGN

There are three considerations to resolve before you can start to build your kiln: (1) power available; (2) the type of ware to be fired; (3) the size of kiln required. These are interdependent, each controlling the other two.

POWER

As a rough guide for an all-purpose kiln, i.e., up to 2300° F. (1260° C.) you need an ample supply of electricity, and it is best to consult with both an electrician and the electric supply company for their requirements. Small kilns using, say, 15 amperes on a 110-volt line, can use the regular electric wiring found in any home or shop. Larger kilns, requiring more amperes, would require special wiring. The same problems arise, of course, whether you build or buy a kiln ready-made. The cost of electric installation also varies with its availability.

TYPE OF WARE

Higher firings entail more efficient installation. It is worth the initial outlay in order to save current over the whole life of the kiln.

If you want to fire stoneware or porcelain, therefore, some 7½ inches of wall is recommended; for lower temperatures 6 inches or even 4 inches with ½-inch asbestos covering may suffice—but err on the generous side.

Similarly, the quality of the wire used for the elements will vary with the maximum temperature required. Nickel chrome elements will suffice for enamels, but you need heavier-duty elements for earthenware and stoneware. Check with your electrician. Connectors, switches, bats, etc., must all correspond with the maximum temperature required.

KILN SIZE

The minimum size for a working kiln would be a 12-inch cube. One twice this volume would be much more efficient. Remember that linear

Illustration 137
Two types of commercially available kilns. Above, a front-loader and, right, a top-loader. A top-loader is the easiest for the home potter to build and is preferred by many potters.

Photographs from "Practical Encyclopedia of Crafts."

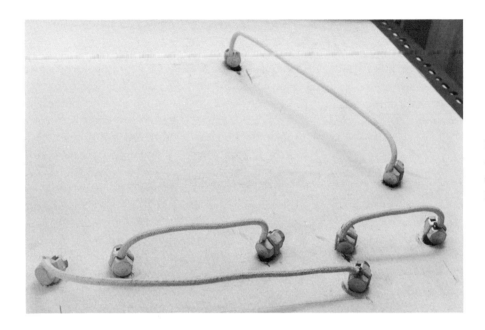

Illustration 138. Asbestos-covered wire is most suitable for withstanding high kiln temperatures.

measurements are misleading, e.g., 12 inches × 12 inches × 12 inches is one cubic foot; 13 inches × 13 inches × 13 inches is one and one-third cubic feet; 15 inches × 15 inches × 15 inches is two cubic feet. It is the cubic volume of the stacking space which counts when estimating heating requirements.

Dimensions should also take into account the available fire-brick sizes. Fire-bricks are available in both standard sizes and grades. The higher the number, the more refractory the brick.

MATERIALS

Bolted angle metal is suitable for the frame. The frame must be capable of bearing the very considerable weight of the finished kiln and so must the floor of the studio or workshop.

The *covering* of the kiln may be of sheet metal or, for more effective insulation, an asbestos-type sheeting. Three-eighths of an inch is a good all around thickness.

The *lining* (outer) bricks can be low temperature insulators with a rating of around 1652° F. (900° C.). The hot-face (inner) bricks must be white, refractory 2552° F. (1400° C.) and easy to cut.

The *elements* will vary according to the ware to be fired, but heavy-duty wire elements are needed to stand a kiln temperature of 2318° F. (1270° C.). For internal *connections* use asbestos-covered wire of suitable gauge for the maximum load and line tap connectors between elements and wire. The ordinary brass and ceramic connectors tend to blacken and corrode under the joint impact of heat and steam.

An *isolator* fused switch box will be necessary and connecting wires between box and kiln should be in a flexible metal sheath. The electrician will have to take care of this.

The kiln *roof* is made up of ¾-inch bats covered over with insulating bricks to the same thickness as the walls. A sheet of ⅜-inch asbestos should go over all.

DESIGN

In planning the kiln, start from the desired muffle size (pot stacking space) and work outwards. A typical plan for a 15 inch × 15 inch × 12 inch capacity would use fourteen 18 inch × 9 inch × 4½ inch slabs (including the roof) and twelve 4½ inch × 3 inch × 9 inch bricks for the corners.

The outer skin would use twenty-six 12 inch × 12 inch × 3 inch low temperature insulating slabs. This would insulate to a standard not often found in the cheaper commercial kiln.

When a plan of the brickwork has been drawn up, it will indicate the frame size. Dry-built construction is recommended with bricks fitting fairly snugly but without joining cement.

Illustration 139

A typical plan for a 15-cubic-inch kiln. Note cut corners of hot-face slabs which effectively lock them together.

THE ELEMENTS

The element to be used depends upon a balance of three variables: the length of the wire, the thickness of wire, and the power available or desired.

The power used and the heat given out by an element depends on the *resistance* it puts up to the flow of current. This resistance is lower in a thick wire than in a thin one (as a rough analogy imagine water running through large and small diameter pipes) but, as each foot of wire exerts its own measure of resistance a short wire will offer less resistance than a long one. It follows that a short fat wire will pass a lot of current and a long thin one much less. Kiln wire diameters in general vary and it is advisable to find out the preferred diameter of several different elements available to determine your needs. The wire will be thicker for a kiln to be fired to stoneware temperatures than for earthenware.

Grooves for elements have to be cut in the

Illustration 140
Element sockets cut in brick. Also shown are positions of elements.

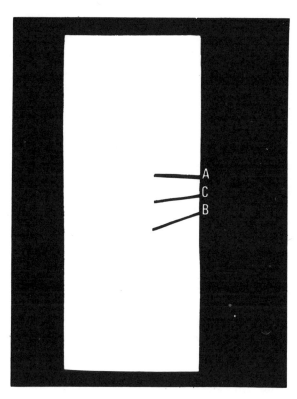

Illustration 141
The three saw cuts for element sockets.

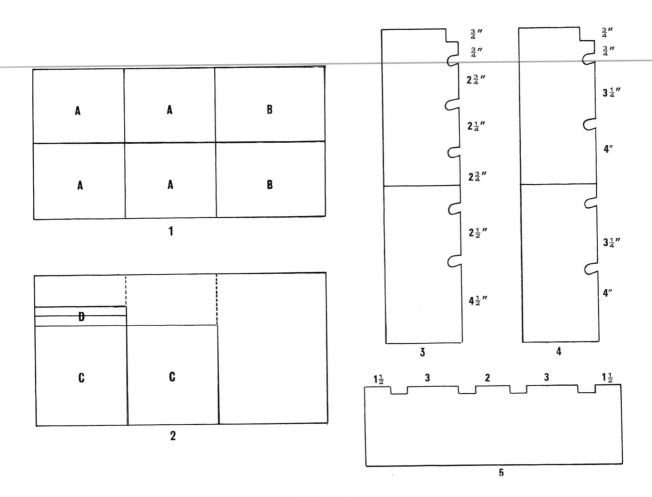

Illustration 142
Cutting plan. See opposite page for description.

face of the brick or slab with an ordinary saw and should be cut wider at the base and slope downwards. The entrance should be just wide enough to accept the wound element. Smooth the groove with a rounded metal tool, such as the handle of a small turning tool.

Electricity is a patient and useful slave, but it also has unlimited energy and must be respected as such. Do not connect any kiln to the mains yourself. It must be suitably grounded and wired by a competent electrician.

With these precautions the kiln will be no more dangerous than a stove or heater. If the kiln is insulated to the degree recommended, the outside should not get too hot to touch even if the inside temperature is 2282° F. (1250° C.)!

BUILDING THE KILN

The kiln illustrated here is designed to reach stoneware temperature 2282° F. (1250° C.), has enough insulation to use current efficiently, requires a minimum cutting of insulating bricks and slabs, and is dry-built and self-supporting. The last factor makes possible future enlargement or alteration and easy dismantling for moving. The effective muffle size is 15 inches × 17 inches × 15 inches high or just over 2 cubic feet.

TOOLS

The abrasive nature of kiln brick, although it is quite easy to work, wears a saw smooth. A cross-cut saw past its best can be used, especially if you can recut the teeth or get this done easily.

For the rest a screwdriver, a monkey wrench for nuts, a plane, a ruler, an 18-inch length of wood 1 inch × 1½ inch or thereabouts, and a pottery turning tool for grouting grooves complete the short list of tools required for this stage of the work.

CUTTING INSTRUCTIONS
(Follow diagrams in Illustration 142.)

ANGLES (metal). Four lengths 37 inches (3 out of a 10 foot piece) for long sides.

Four lengths 30 inches (4 out of a 10-foot piece) for crosspieces.

Four lengths 29 inches (4 out of a 10-foot piece) for uprights.

One length 34 inches (this and one 37-inch long side out of a fourth 10-foot piece) for floor diagonal.

ASBESTOS. Two 8-foot × 4-foot sheets cut as Diagrams 1 and 2.

Key to diagrams:

A. End walls and connector covers. Four pieces each 24 inches × 30 inches.

B. Long sides. Two pieces each 24 inches × 36 inches.

C. Top cover and base sheet. Two pieces each 30 inches × 32 inches.

D. Top of connector covers. Two pieces each 30 inches × 3 inches.

BRICKS. Apart from element slots and 12 rebates, all refractories are of regular shape and many of them remain the standard size: 18 inches × 9 inches × 4½ inches and 12 inches × 12 inches × 3 inches "slabs," and 9 inches × 3 inches × 4½ inches "bricks."

A preliminary fitting of the white refractories entails the following:

One slab cut to 15 inches × 9 inches (for floor).

One slab cut to 15 inches × 8 inches (for floor).

Two bricks cut to 8 inches long (for floor surround).

Eight bricks cut to 9 inches × 3 inches × 4 inches (½-inch slice off side) for corner uprights.

All other slabs remain 18 inches × 9 inches (× 4½ inches).

Four slabs have rebates cut in opposite 9-inch sides, ½-inch from face and 1½ inches from sides.

Fit the white refractories together to form a hollow cube, measuring 24 inches × 26 inches × 21 inches high. It is made up of 10 slabs (four with the rebates mentioned above), 17 bricks, and two 1½-inch fillers in the surround to the muffle floor. For the arrangement of the floor bricks see Illustration 143. The walls of the muffle are rigid and cannot move inwards although no joining material is used. Number the pieces so that they can go back in the same place and dismantle. The plane can be used for fitting bricks which may not lie flush, but there should be little necessity for this at this stage.

OUTER LINING. All are full size except for: Three slabs cut to 12 inches × 8 inches.

Two of the 12-inch × 4-inch pieces left will make up a fourth, 12 inches × 8 inches.

One 12-inch × 4-inch piece (remaining from above) is cut into two 12-inch × 2-inch pieces to fill floor gaps.

These slabs do not have the precision of the inner-face ones and will need planing to achieve a reasonably snug fit.

ELEMENT GROOVES
AND ROOF BAT FITTING

Lay two appropriate slabs together and measure and mark the element grooves as shown in 3 and 4 in Illustration 142. In the diagrams, measurements are those *between*

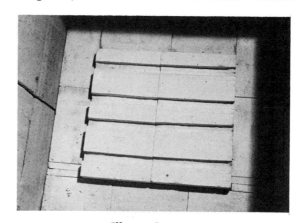

Illustration 143
Floor of muffle and surrounding bricks.

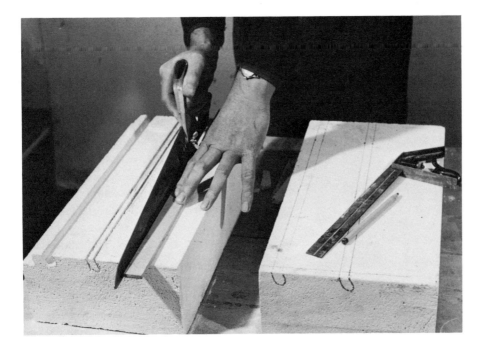

Illustration 144. Fire-brick slabs marked for grooves. An upper cut being sawed.

grooves; the grooves in the walls are ½ inch wide at the entrance, those in the floor 1 inch wide and ½ inch deep. The five element walls are the long 17-inch walls; the four element walls are the rebated 15-inch walls.

Two saw cuts are then made for each groove, both sloping inwards towards the bottom of the brick (as it will stand in the kiln) the lower cut being at the more acute angle. Use the wood slat as a guide to start the cut. With the saw in the second (lower) cut, press the blade towards the upper cut. The strip of brick will snap and can be lifted out. Next take the turning tool and, holding it well in the slot and slightly at an angle, scrape out a rounded base to the groove.

For the roof bat, the top of each wall must be rebated so that the bat will fit flush within the top of the kiln wall. The roof bat will measure $16\frac{3}{8}$ inches $\times$ $18\frac{3}{4}$ inches $\times$ $\frac{3}{4}$ inch.

Illustration 145. Grouting a groove with turning tool.

Illustration 146
Inner cube partially assembled.

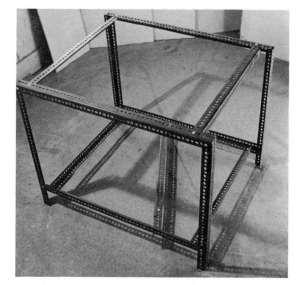

Illustration 147
The frame bolted together.

ASSEMBLY INSTRUCTIONS

Bolt the frame together and check the measurements. The cube should be 33 inches × 31 inches × 24 inches deep. It will be found that the frame members must be pulled out to the maximum size the bolt holes will permit. Illustrations 147–148 show the frame complete and a closeup of the crosspiece joins where a gap is essential to take the asbestos sheet. The 30-inch lengths will be seen to be cut very close to a hole.

Next fit the asbestos. It will be necessary to unfasten one upright on each side to slide in the 36-inch sheets. The rest will slip in with a

bit of juggling. In some cases, especially with the 36-inch × 24-inch sheets the corners will have to be cut across to avoid bolts.

The kiln is now ready for the red slabs. As previously mentioned, some planing will be involved. Arrange the upper layer so that sound, smooth edges show around the top. The longer walls are made up of four full-size slabs and two 12 inches × 8 inches; the shorter sides of four full slabs; and the floor of four full slabs and two 12 inches × 2 inches. The surface of the slabs must be cut away wherever a bolt protrudes.

Illustration 148
Corner of frame with gap for insulation.

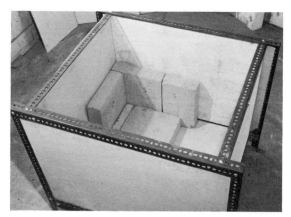

Illustration 149
Insulation sheets in place and slabs in position.

Illustration 150
Outer lining nearly complete.

Illustration 151
Last slab being inserted.

Lastly, the white hot-face cube is built in, the last four slabs sliding in from above. The electric kiln box is now complete. The left-over fire-bricks and slabs are for the lid. You should have nothing wasted except the groove bits and an awful lot of brick dust.

Do not finally assemble the inner box until all minor grooves are made to accommodate the hairpin bends of the elements.

Have an electrician wire the kiln for you, if you do not know all the necessary details for this, and then complete the assembly of the inner wall of the kiln.

FINAL ASSEMBLY

In the final stages of assembly, bolt on the asbestos end panels to protect the connections and fix narrow strips across the top. Two semi-circular finger grip holes should be cut into each side of the ¾-inch lid bat.

The peephole also must be cut. To cut it, drill from the inside between two slots (not too near the bottom of a slot or the element may sag). Then, working mainly from the outside, enlarge the hole to a convenient shape. Throw a clay piece at the wheel to fit.

Illustration 152. Laying roofing bats on kiln. Note high temperature insulating blocks put on to cover top of kiln at each firing.

Illustration 153
Top of kiln with roof in position.

PROCEDURES

In building a kiln, always remember to follow these guidelines.

• Check to see that no connections or bare wires are in danger of touching one another or, especially, *any part of the metal framework* before switching on the kiln for the first time.

• Don't switch the kiln on for the first time until an electrician has checked all of the wiring. Later on, do not switch on until you are sure that *all connections* and the *lid bat* are in position.

• *Keep the overall length of each circuit constant* or the current load will be altered.

Illustration 154
Complete frame and brick.

109

ABOUT THE AUTHOR

Robert Charles Privett Fournier has his own pottery in England and is a Full Craft Member of three organizations: the Craftsmen Potters Association of Great Britain (as well as a Council Member of that Association), the Craft Centre of Great Britain and the Red Rose Guild of Craftsmen.

His work has been exhibited in London at the Alan Malcolm Gallery, at the University of Sussex, at the Gardner Centre for the Arts, and at various English festivals and smaller galleries.

He has been a Craftsman Potter since 1947, and is now a full-time potter. He has taught at the Maidstone College of Art and several other schools and given an extensive series of lectures on the techniques of ceramics, including twenty-four consecutive lectures on the complete history of the craft. Besides writing books and magazine articles for CANVAS Magazine, he is making and issuing professional films and slides on ceramics.

Mr. Fournier has built all his own equipment —wheels, kilns, etc.—and constructed the first house and pottery in Hertfordshire from the ground up. He has a large collection of modern craft pottery and some antiquities. His next book will be on teaching ceramics.

Illustration 155
A ceramic flower arrangement trough.

Index